365 Daily
Prayers and
Declarations
for Women

BroadStreet
PUBLISHING

BroadStreet Publishing Group, LLC.
Savage, Minnesota, USA
Broadstreetpublishing.com

365 DAILY PRAYERS AND DECLARATIONS FOR WOMEN
© 2022 by BroadStreet Publishing®

978-1-4245-6402-6
978-1-4245-6403-3 (eBook)

Devotional entries composed by Sara Perry and Suzanne Niles. Compiled by Michelle Winger.

Design and typesetting by Garborg Design Works | garborgdesign.com

Printed in China.

22   23   24   25   26   27   28   7   6   5   4   3   2   1

The earnest prayer of
a righteous person
has great power
and produces
wonderful results.

JAMES 5:16 NLT

Introduction

"The earth and sky will wear out and fade away before one word I speak loses its power or fails to accomplish its purpose."

MATTHEW 24:35 TPT

This is one of the many promises God has spoken over you. His promises are for every situation and for all time. They reflect his character and confirm his purpose for your life.

This book of prayers and declarations will help you gain confidence in the never-ending love and mercy of God. When you need encouragement or a reminder of who God is, turn to his Word and declare it over your situation. God's Word is living and active and as relevant today as it was when it was written.

As you reflect on these daily entries, grab hold of God's promises, declare them over your life, and discover his unlimited grace and strength.

January

The earnest prayer of a
righteous person has
great power and produces
wonderful results.

JAMES 5:16 NLT

True Delight

What delight comes to the one
who follows God's ways!

PSALM 1:1 TPT

Father of wisdom, I don't want to ever lose sight of the joy that is found in your presence. Surround me with your Spirit and fill my heart with your peace that passes understanding. Though I find delight in many areas of my life, not one is as sweet as the delight I find in your affection.

As I follow you on the path of your loving kindness, throwing aside my judgments and worries, I trust that your joyful peace will be my portion. Thank you for loving me so wholly. I delight in you freely because of your unfailing mercy.

I declare that as I go about my day, I will choose to walk in the wisdom of God's ways. As I choose mercy over judgment and kindness over shutting down in offense, I will find greater freedom in your love. Instead of preserving myself and my own preferences, I will choose to consider the effects my actions have on those around me. By God's grace, I will live more openly, with compassion as my motivation.

Never-ending Mercy

He delivered us from such a deadly peril, and he will deliver us. On him we have set our hope that he will deliver us again.

2 CORINTHIANS 1:10 ESV

Great God, you are my deliverer. You are the one I put my hope in when every other hopeful possibility has dissipated. You are the strength I desperately need when I am too weak to stand on my own. When the world around me is chaotic and feels as if it's closing in on me, you are my only hope.

I long for your confident peace to surround me and flood my senses. Deliver me, Lord! Free me from my fears and rescue me from crippling anxiety. I cling to you; I trust in you. Come, Lord, once again.

Just as you have already done for others, I declare that your love will surround and meet me in the midst of my messiest circumstances. You are the deliverer, and you will never change. I declare that my heart can trust in you completely, for you have done great things. You are not finished working your mercy.

Unshakeable Faith

If your faith remains strong, even while surrounded by life's difficulties, you will continue to experience the untold blessings of God! True happiness comes as you pass the test with faith, and receive the victorious crown of life promised to every lover of God!

JAMES 1:12 TPT

Jesus, I put my faith completely in your character and in your unending mercy. I don't need all the answers to trust you. Strong faith is built upon the foundation of your goodness, not my own, and I am so thankful for that. There is nothing I could do to convince you to love me more; you already love me through and through.

I build my hope around your nature, and I give you access to my heart. I lay down my worries and my cares, and I stand upon your Word. Even as life's challenges continue, I will keep believing that you are good, you are faithful, and you are true.

I declare that even when difficulties surround me the goodness of the Lord never falters. I put my faith in the Creator of all things, and I stand upon the truth of his unending mercy. As I go about my day, I will see the power of his Spirit at work in my life, bringing fruit of patience, peace, and joy even when that shouldn't naturally be the case. The Lord is my victory.

Rescued

He has rescued us from the kingdom of darkness and transferred us into the Kingdom of his dear Son.

COLOSSIANS 1:13 NLT

King of kings, there is no way I can begin to adequately thank you for your incredible kindness toward me. Thank you for rescuing me from the darkness I was once in and bringing me into your glorious light. Here, I have found a home in your peace, and I have come alive in your life-giving love.

Thank you for the freedom I have in you. Nothing that can overpower the strength of your mercy! You have given me space to run, to breathe deeply, and to heal. Thank you for calling me your own.

Today in the light of this moment, I declare that the freedom I knew at first in Christ is the same powerful freedom I have right here and now. In the power of Christ, I am free to live in his love. There is nothing that can separate me from his powerful mercy, and no one can take his love away from me. I have been delivered from fear's threats, and I belong to the King of kings.

Unchangeable God

Every good action and every perfect gift is from God. These good gifts come down from the Creator of the sun, moon, and stars, who does not change like their shifting shadows.

JAMES 1:17 NCV

Unchangeable One, when I see how the sun reflects off a mountainside as it sets, when I feel the breeze of the ocean on my face and hear the sound of its crashing waves, I can't help but be in awe of your workmanship. You, the God who created wildflowers and shooting stars, are the same God who cares for me.

Thank you for the perfect gifts of your goodness in my life. Give me eyes to see the beauty of the mundane, for I know that you are as present in my dullest moments as you are in the most exhilarating. I love you!

As I go about my day, I declare that my eyes will be open to the gifts of God's goodness all around me. I will not miss a detail of the perfection that is already present in my life and that rises to meet me. I will walk in this world filled with compassion and curiosity, and I will grow in my capacity for wonder and awe as I notice God's fingerprints in creation.

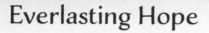
Everlasting Hope

The hope of eternal life, which God, who does not lie, promised before the beginning of time.

TITUS 1:2 NIV

Lord, I believe that you are the way, the truth, and the life. I trust that what you said is true and that you will do it. You are unchanging in loyal love to all you have made, and I am included in that.

Thank you for the promise of your kingdom and the unshakeable hope of everlasting life in the living light of your presence. Encourage my heart by your Spirit today and fill me with the confidence of your presence. You are my hope, and I cling to you.

I declare that no matter what I'm facing today, no matter what I'm going through, God is the same powerful, good, loving, saving God that he has always been. I have no need to fear, for the hope of his coming kingdom is my foundation and will not be shaken. No matter how many days I have in this one short life, there is more to look forward to in the next.

In Christ

The yes to all of God's promises is in Christ,
and through Christ we say yes to the glory of God.

2 CORINTHIANS 1:20 NCV

Lord Jesus, in you I find the fullness of God's heart of love. You who spent time with the outcasts, who dined with tax collectors, and who wandered from town to town sharing the love of the Father, you are the one I look to today. I'm so grateful that you are not easily offended.

I am drawn to your love, and I am pierced by your truth. Thank you for showing us what the Father's heart looks like. You are the way, the truth, and the life.

I declare that in your love I am made whole. You are my freedom, my peace, and my joy. There is no one else who loves me so completely, who lifts me up when I am beaten down by life, or who consistently stays by my side. I declare that every good and perfect gift is from you. You are my greatest treasure.

Divine Clues

Ever since the world was created,
people have seen the earth and sky.
Through everything God made,
they can clearly see his invisible qualities—
his eternal power and divine nature.
So they have no excuse for not knowing God.

ROMANS 1:20 NLT

Creator, I see your workmanship in the intricacy of the world around me. There is so much beauty in the construction of snowflakes, and wonder rises within my heart when I watch the light and colors change in a beautiful sunset.

As I marvel at creation, my heart grows in its desire to know you more. Reveal your loving kindness to me in fresh ways as I look to you today. Fill me with awe and wonder as you expand my understanding of your great kindness. I long to know you more.

Even as the stars shine bright in the velvet blanket of the sky, I declare that your light shines brighter in me. I am a reflection of your life-giving mercy, and it glows brighter than the sun. As I look at the world around me, I will not miss the beauty of your character and creativity.

Endless Opportunities

When troubles of any kind come your way,
consider it an opportunity for great joy.
For you know that when your faith is tested,
your endurance has a chance to grow.

JAMES 1:2-3 NLT

Great God, thank you for the opportunity to reframe my experiences in the light of your great love. No trouble is too difficult for you, and I know that each one is an opportunity to experience your abiding presence in even greater measure.

You are my joy, and the development of my character reflects your work in my life. Give me patient endurance and the tenacity to keep holding on to your perspective and truth over my own understanding. I open my heart to you again.

I declare that no matter what I face today, I will do it with the strength of the Spirit of God as my sustenance and source. Nothing can keep me from the great and merciful heart of my Father. Even in the greatest struggles and most inconvenient interruptions, I will find an opportunity to press into the joy of the Lord.

Kept by God

All glory to God, who is able to keep you from falling away and will bring you with great joy into his glorious presence without a single fault.

JUDE 1:24 NLT

Merciful Father, thank you for your faithfulness in my life. I rely on your power to keep me close, your peace to comfort my wavering heart, and your joy to be my strength. Thank you for surrounding me with your presence and for leading me into deeper freedom in your love.

You are the one who keeps me from falling. You are the hope I hold on to, and even more importantly, you hold on to me with your unending mercy. There is nothing that intimidates you, and I am so relieved to know that you see all things clearly. In you, there is hope for restoration and redemption.

I declare that no matter the temptation I've had to give up, God is not finished with me yet. He is not discouraged or disheartened by the things that discourage me. There is more joy, more peace, more passion, more love, and more hope in the abundant presence of Christ within me.

Greater Wisdom

The foolishness of God is wiser than human wisdom, and the weakness of God is stronger than human strength.

1 CORINTHIANS 1:25 NIV

Wise God, there is no greater perspective in the universe than yours. Being the source of all life, you see everything clearly. Nothing stumps you. Thank you for sharing your wisdom with those who seek it. I long to know you more and to walk in the fullness of your kingdom.

As I look to you today, give me greater revelation of your ways. Fill me with the strength of your presence. In light of the perspective of your greatness, I am as miniscule as an ant. Even so, you offer me access to your unmatched wisdom. Thank you!

I open myself up to the direction, discernment, and wisdom of God today. I will not rely on my own understanding but on the perspective of God who rules and reigns over all. As I look to his Word and meditate on the Scriptures, I will find direction and guidance. I declare that God's wisdom rules my life.

Everything We Need

By his divine power, God has given us everything we need for living a godly life. We have received all of this by coming to know him, the one who called us to himself by means of his marvelous glory and excellence.

2 PETER 1:3 NLT

Glorious One, I look to you for all my needs. Every lack is a reminder to turn to you. You don't hesitate to meet me with the provision of your presence. You don't withhold what I need. The roots of my faith are deeply planted in your mercy, and I want to live by drawing strength directly from the source of your pure and living waters.

Open my eyes to see where you have already met my needs. Give me greater assurance and peace in my heart to trust that you will continue to do it.

As a child of God, I am no stranger to his goodness. He does not withhold his abundance from me; he overwhelms my needs with the riches of his glory. He is more powerful than my fears, and I will continue to see the goodness of my God in the land of the living.

Living Hope

Blessed be the God and Father of our Lord Jesus Christ! According to his great mercy, he has caused us to be born again to a living hope through the resurrection of Jesus Christ from the dead, to an inheritance that is imperishable, undefiled, and unfading, kept in heaven for you.

1 Peter 1:3-4 esv

Merciful Father, thank you for the living hope I find in your Son. Through the resurrection power of his sacrifice, I have been made alive in your love. Though trials and troubles come and sometimes overwhelm me, I will not forget that you are the Redeemer, the restorer and lifter of my head.

Lift the worries that have weighed down my hope as I open my hands to you in surrender. I offer you the heavy load of my fears. Deliver me into your joy and your peace once more as I fix my eyes on Jesus, my true and living hope.

No matter what I face today, my inheritance in Christ is undiminished. Nothing can keep me from the love of God, and no one can steal my destiny. I am firmly held within the mercy of God's heart, and my future is established in him. Praise God!

True Comfort

Praise be to the God and Father of our Lord Jesus Christ. God is the Father who is full of mercy and all comfort. He comforts us every time we have trouble, so when others have trouble, we can comfort them with the same comfort God gives us.

2 CORINTHIANS 1:3-4 NCV

Comforter, thank you for coming close in my trouble and for drawing near to me in my heartbreak. When discouragement weighs down my heart, you are ever so close. Wrap around me with the loving kindness of your presence. Settle my anxiety with your soothing peace.

I lean back into your love, pressing more keenly into this moment where you meet me as I am. Thank you for your mercy that does not diminish or increase based on my feelings. It is always abundant.

I will offer praise to God today for his nearness. Even in my discomfort, his peace is available. In my great grief, his Spirit is near and comforts me. I declare that I will not look to escape the pain of my emotions; instead, I will allow God to minister to me in them.

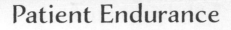

Patient Endurance

Let patience have its perfect work,
that you may be perfect and complete,
lacking nothing.

JAMES 1:4 NKJV

Perfect One, you know me better than I know myself. You see how I struggle to slow down in the waiting and to let each moment have its significance. I would rather rush ahead into the exciting parts of life than settle into the rhythms of ebb and flow.

But you, oh God, created the seasons, and you put the rhythms of nature into place. I want to value what you value and allow myself to sink into the periods of waiting and tending that promote greater growth. I trust you more than I trust my own senses.

Where I feel hurried, instead of continuing to rush ahead, I will slow down into the moment and ask myself why I feel the need to move so quickly. There is beauty in process, and I will learn to love it. I declare that I will let patience produce maturity, presence, and pleasure in the little things. I will start today!

Holy Spirit Help

We know, brothers and sisters loved by God, that he has chosen you, because our gospel came to you not simply with words but also with power, with the Holy Spirit and deep conviction. You know how we lived among you for your sake.

1 Thessalonians 1:4-5 niv

Holy Spirit, without your help, all I have is knowledge and a set of belief systems. I don't want to rely only on words that others have spoken. Produce deeper conviction in my heart as you draw near and fill my life with the power of your presence. I want to know you as I know my closest friends. I want to fellowship with you, to be astounded by you, and to know the love of God more fully through your friendship.

There is nothing I withhold from you. Walk with me, teach me, and fill me with your fruit. I yield to you.

I declare that my life will not simply be marked by what I say I believe but also by the power of God at work within me. The Holy Spirit teaches me through revelation and deeper wisdom in my innermost being. As the Word of God comes alive, my whole being vibrates with the radiance of his love, joy, peace, and hope.

Pure Light

This is the message we have heard from him and declare to you: God is light; in him there is no darkness at all.

1 JOHN 1:5 NIV

Radiant One, in the light of your presence, I come alive. There are no hidden agendas within your heart, and there is no trickery in your approach to humanity. You are full of loyal love, reaching out in mercy and grace to all. Thank you for loving me so completely, for freeing me of my shame, and for giving me your abundant peace when the world is unsteady.

As I look to you for wisdom, the pure light of your truth shines on my understanding. Radiant God, shine on me with the brilliant light of your kindness once again. Fill me to overflow with the joy of your presence. I long to catch a greater glimpse of your glory today.

In the light of God's presence, all shadows are illuminated. I declare that as I live with intention and a surrendered heart to him, there is nothing to fear. All wrongs will be made right in him, and he will not let darkness destroy me.

Compelling Love

Because of his love, God had already decided to make us his own children through Jesus Christ. That was what he wanted and what pleased him.

EPHESIANS 1:5 NCV

Loving Father, I can't begin to imagine or describe the lengths of your compassion. My mind can't comprehend the immensity of your mercy. Love compels all you do. Jesus described you and displayed your loyal and gracious love, and it wiped away visions of a hard-to-please deity who was out of touch with our pain and suffering.

Jesus revealed you as the tender and patient father to the prodigal son. He demonstrated your great compassion through healing those that society had deemed unclean, untouchable, and unlovable. Everyone has a home in your love. Thank you, Father!

I declare that there is no reason to let fear keep me stuck in cycles of regret and shame when love has already set me free. The Father is not disappointed in me, so why would I let my own disappointment keep me from coming to him? I am his dearly loved child, and I run to his arms today.

Generous Wisdom

If any of you needs wisdom, you should ask God for it.
He is generous to everyone and will give you wisdom
without criticizing you.

JAMES 1:5 NCV

Wise God, I come to you with all my questions, my
wonderings, and my doubts today. I believe that you are
generous with your perspective as well as your love. Teach
me your ways, lead me into your wisdom, and keep me
steady in your truth.

You know how much I need your input in my life. I will not
despise the need to ask, for you are full of wisdom and see
everything clearly. I rely on your fellowship, and I delight in
receiving revelations of your perspective that broaden my
own. Your wisdom expands my understanding while fear
keeps me thinking small. Generous God, teach me more of
your ways today.

*More than I want my own way, I want to walk in the wisdom
of God's ways. I want to pursue the path of love that Jesus
set out. I declare that God's wisdom is my guiding light. I
will not walk blindly; he illuminates the steps before me.*

Chosen

"Before I formed you in the womb I knew you,
before you were born I set you apart."

JEREMIAH 1:5 NIV

Creator, thank you for knowing me better than any
other. You know what makes me curious, what drives my
ambition, and what holds me back in fear. You know every
motivation of my heart and the number of hairs on my
head. You, my Creator, formed me in my mother's womb.
Even before you did it, you knew who I would become.

I trust that you do not make mistakes and that who I am
is wonderful to you. I yield my heart and life to yours
knowing that you are the one who always knows best. Lead
me in your love and shine your light on me. I want to come
alive in the delight of your presence.

*I am beautifully and wonderfully made. I declare that I will
accept and cherish who I am as much as God does, for
the one who created me delights in his children. I have
been chosen as his own, so I will live in the freedom and
confidence of his love.*

He's Still Working

I am sure of this, that he who began a good work in you
will bring it to completion at the day of Jesus Christ.

PHILIPPIANS 1:6 ESV

Perfect God, thank you for never giving up on me. Even
when I can't see what you are doing, I believe that your
mercy is weaving through the fabric of my life. Encourage
my heart today in the truth that you are not finished
with me yet. Today is not the end of my story; it is a new
opportunity and a continuation of your faithfulness.

Give me eyes to see where you are already moving in
mighty ways. Let your power revive my heart in hope. May
the peace of your presence guard my mind and settle my
heart today.

*I declare that the work that the Lord has started in me is
his to finish. He is not done working miracles of his mercy
through my story. This moment is all I have, and here he
meets me with the fullness of his presence. I am wholly
loved, fully accepted, and wonderfully set free right here
and now in his perfect love.*

Trust Him

Be truly glad! There is wonderful joy ahead. You love him even though you have never seen him. Though you do not see him now, you trust him; and you rejoice with a glorious, inexpressible joy.

1 PETER 1:6, 8-9 NLT

Trustworthy One, thank you for the joy I find in your presence. I'm grateful that there's more joy promised ahead. I have tasted and seen your goodness in my life, and yet I long for so much more. I long for a fresh drink of your mercy that meets me right where I am.

Fill me with your presence and surround me with your light and life. Expand my understanding in your wisdom and breathe relief into the deep recesses of my soul as I release what I can't control to your hands. I trust you.

I declare that God is worthy of my trust no matter the circumstances I face. Though storms may come and go, his Word remains true. His mercy is immovable and abundant toward me. I will continue to press into his peace as I surrender my trust to him over and over again.

Light of Unity

If we keep living in the pure light that surrounds him, we share unbroken fellowship with one another, and the blood of Jesus, his Son, continually cleanses us from all sin.

1 JOHN 1:7 TPT

Radiant Jesus, I long to live in the light of your presence all the days of my life. I want to choose love rather than nursing my offenses. I want to be a promoter of peace rather than a sower of dissension.

As I look to you now, shine the light of your loving grace over my mind, in my heart, and through my entire being. Make me one with you. May all shame, fear, and worries be silenced by our present peace. Thank you!

No matter how often I fall and fail, there is always a fresh opportunity to rise again. The pure light of Jesus' presence is right here with me, and it has not diminished. I am made whole in his loving embrace, and there is nothing that his mercy leaves untouched in my life. I am one with him and unified with those who fellowship with him.

Purified and Strengthened

These trials will show that your faith is genuine. It is
being tested as fire tests and purifies gold—though your
faith is far more precious than mere gold. So when your
faith remains strong through many trials, it will bring
you much praise and glory and honor on the day when
Jesus Christ is revealed to the whole world.

1 PETER 1:7 NLT

Faithful Father, I will not let the pressures of life keep me
from turning to you today. You are my perfect portion,
my source of hope, and all I need to inspire me to keep
choosing the path of love.

Flood my senses with your empowering presence and lead
me in your mercy. I know that trials will come and go, but
your steadfast love will never cease. Strengthen me and
purify me as I continue to press into you. I rely on your help
and your leadership, Lord.

*My faith is strengthened by the presiding passion to keep
going no matter what. Even as struggles remain in my life,
endurance is built in my soul as I press into the present
peace of God. I will continue to give God access to my
heart and life because he is my hope.*

Spirit of Self-control

God gave us a spirit not of fear but of power and love and self-control.

2 TIMOTHY 1:7 ESV

Spirit, you are full of all good and heavenly gifts. Your presence brings peace, joy, comfort, strength, hope, and love. You give perspective to my closed-mindedness, and you broaden my understanding with the revelations of God's true nature. You are my confidant, my closest friend, and my best help. Without you, I don't know what I would do! You fill me with clarity for my confusion, and you give space to make conscious choices when I feel rushed.

Thank you for your fellowship. Without it, I would be lost. Thank you for your love that settles my fears and calms my anxieties. Here, I am able to make loving and wise decisions in light of your kingdom values.

I have the Spirit of peace, love, and self-control residing within me. He is my guiding light, my greatest advisor, and the voice of truth. I will not rush forward, stay stuck, or run away in fear. I will stand my ground and allow the Spirit of love to free me from the shackles of shame that inhibit me. I am free indeed in the presence of Jesus.

Generous Kindness

He is so rich in kindness and grace that he purchased our freedom with the blood of his Son and forgave our sins.

EPHESIANS 1:7 NLT

Jesus, thank you for the generous kindness of your sacrifice. You are better than I could put words to, and your promise of freedom in your mercy is the greatest gift I have ever received. You are full of generosity. Your joy, peace, love, kindness, strength, and hope are more plentiful than I can imagine.

Fill me with fresh revelations of the lengths of your love. I want to worship you in wonder today. I will not forget the grace that you openhandedly pour out into my life like an unending stream. How I love you!

There is nothing in my life that is hidden from Jesus or his mercy. He purchased my freedom, and I am truly alive in his love. There is no shame, no sin, no addiction, and no compromise that is not covered by his mercy. I have been set free in the merciful tide of his love, and I am truly free.

Always Good

The Lord is good,
a refuge in times of trouble.
He cares for those who trust in him.

NAHUM 1:7 NIV

Lord, you are my safe place. You are my shelter when the storms of life are raging. You are my anchor of hope that holds me when the winds whip about me. You are my loving caregiver and my tender Father. I rely on you to keep me close even as I hunker down in the cellars of your abundance.

Refresh me with the coolness of your refuge. Calm me in the recesses of your goodness. I trust you with all I am, all I have, and all I hope for. You are good.

No matter what is going on in the world around me, I believe that God is good. I declare that I will continue to see the goodness of the Lord in my life. He won't stop working his mercy into the details of my story. I will proclaim with my very life that God is good and that I belong to him.

Spirit Power

You will receive power
when the Holy Spirit comes on you.

ACTS 1:8 NIV

Holy Spirit, I ask you to descend upon my life in greater measure today. Open my ears to hear you and my eyes to see where you are working. I want to know you more, to breathe in the peace of your presence, and to walk in the confidence of your fellowship and friendship. With you as my wise guide, I will not falter to the right or to the left.

Keep my heart entrenched in your abundant and living love. Heal me, restore me, lead me, and challenge me. Soothe my worries and corral my cares with your wise mercy. Move in my life, for I rely on you to do what I could never on my own.

I am a child of the living God, and as such, I am filled with his Spirit. I have yielded my life to Jesus Christ, and he has offered me his presence to help me in every way. I have the power of God at work in my life! I walk in the authority of his name, and I will see even greater things than I have yet experienced in his miracles among us.

Be Encouraged

"Don't be afraid of the people,
for I will be with you and will protect you.
I, the Lord, have spoken!"

JEREMIAH 1:8 NLT

Lord God, you are my hope and my holy encouragement.
You shield me from the accusations of the enemy, and you
are my defender and my advocate. You are the only one
who can move mountains, and today I ask that you do that
in my life.

Encourage my heart in your presence. As I go about my
day, show me in tangible ways that you are with me.
You said that you would never leave or forsake me, and
I believe it. Keep me safe and secure and remove the
barriers that would keep me stuck and small in fear and
shame. Your love is greater than all things.

*I am covered in the favor of God, for I am his beloved child.
I declare that I walk in the freedom of his love and mercy. I
am no prisoner of fear because Christ has set me free. I am
free to live with confidence, for the Lord my God goes with
me into every battle.*

Beginning and End

"I am the Alpha and the Omega,"
says the Lord God,
"who is, and who was, and who is to come,
the Almighty."

REVELATION 1:8 NIV

Almighty God, your existence is outside of time, and I can't begin to imagine the greatness of your being. Though I try to understand the extent of your reach, my mind can't comprehend it.

I worship you, Eternal One, in spirit and in truth. I offer you my life, my trust, and my allegiance. Though there are a multitude of beginnings and endings in this life, there is none in you, and I am grateful for that. Reveal your glory to me in a new way. I want to catch a glimpse I've never seen before.

No one can compare to the Lord of all the earth. I declare that in his eternal love I have found my home; I have no need to look for my place outside of it. The one who was, who is, and who is to come is the same one who created me and called me his own.

Confess and Be Clean

If we confess our sins, He is faithful and just to forgive us our sins and to cleanse us from all unrighteousness.

1 JOHN 1:9 NKJV

Faithful God, thank you for the mercy of your heart that you freely offer me. When I come to you and lay my heart bare before you, you do not condemn or scold me. There are no lectures in your presence. There is only love, acceptance, mercy, and truth. You cover the stain of my regrets with the robes of your righteousness, and I am made clean.

Thank you for cleansing me and setting me free from the shame that threatened to choke the life out of me. You are so much better than anyone I've ever known. Your motives are pure, and your power is limitless.

As I confess my faults, my wrongdoings, and my compromises against love to the Lord, he removes the barriers between him and me. His love is a rushing river that sweeps over the dust of my regrets and brings new life and opportunity. How wonderful it is to be free!

February

Look to the Lord
and his strength;
seek his face always.

1 Chronicles 16:11 niv

Courageous Hope

"Have I not commanded you? Be strong and courageous. Do not be afraid; do not be discouraged, for the Lord your God will be with you wherever you go."

JOSHUA 1:9 NIV

God, you know how weak I am and how susceptible I am to worry. No matter what I fear, you never change. You are as reliable as you were when you parted the Red Sea for the Israelites to escape the army of their enemies. You are as constant today as you were then. You are capable of powerful miracles.

I will not be afraid. Even when I am, I will not let it keep me from following you. I will continue to walk with you, knowing that you are a good God and a faithful leader. I believe that you will continue to move in mighty miracles of mercy as I courageously walk in the way you have prepared.

I declare that where fear has kept me silent, courage loosens my voice. I will not let fear of what others may think, do, or say keep me from walking in the fullness of God's ways. He has set me free, and he will always provide a way for me. I forge ahead in hope.

Preserved by Love

You have granted me life and steadfast love,
and your care has preserved my spirit.

JOB 10:12 ESV

Father, your love preserves my soul and brings me to life from the inside out. You have given me all I need for life; everything I have originated in you. Even my very breath is because you first breathed life into my being. You created me in my mother's womb, and I here I am today, your beloved child still.

Thank you for your tender care that promotes my growth, instructs me in my weakness, and fills me with courage to live unashamed in your mercy. I owe you my very life. All I am and all I have is from you. I am yours!

I declare that I am covered by the unending love of God every day of my life. I am never without the help of God, the source of all things. Everything I am belongs to him, and he will continue to care for me.

A Way Out

The temptations in your life are no different from what others experience. And God is faithful. He will not allow the temptation to be more than you can stand. When you are tempted, he will show you a way out so that you can endure.

1 Corinthians 10:13 NLT

Powerful One, thank you for not leaving me to my own way even when I forge into the wilderness of life without waiting for you. You are greater than my fears, and you will never leave me to fight battles on my own. Thank you for being a sure and steady help, a place of wisdom and retreat.

When I call, you answer. When I am faced with temptations that seem too great to pass up, empower me with your Spirit to choose your way over my own. Show me the way out so I can endure. Raise me up in your love.

I declare that no temptation is my master. Tempting offers do not have power over my choices. I get a fresh choice every single time I face a decision. I am led by love, and love won't lead me to destruction. I trust the wisdom of my God more than I trust the leanings of my heart.

Perfected by Christ

With one sacrifice he made perfect forever
those who are being made holy.

HEBREWS 10:14 NCV

Christ Jesus, you are the way, the truth, and the life. I come
to you, and through you, I find who the Father is. He is
good, merciful, and full of radiant light. In you, I find myself
completely and totally at home. Here, I am surrounded
by your plentiful peace, your brilliant joy, and your
uncompromising hope.

I don't have to be perfect, and for that I can never stop
thanking you. There is so much more grace than I could
outrun. I give you all my hopes, all my dreams, and all my
longings. You, Lord Jesus, are my perfection. You are my
hope, and you are my home.

*I am perfected by the sacrifice of Jesus. Nothing I do could
add or take away from what he has already done on the
cross. I am not a slave to sin, shame, or fear. I am free to
live a life of love in all my messy humanity.*

He Sees

You, God, see the trouble of the afflicted;
you consider their grief and take it in hand.
The victims commit themselves to you;
you are the helper of the fatherless.

PSALM 10:14 NIV

Holy One, the disappointments of life can sometimes feel too much to bear. When loss sweeps through my life, I can barely stand on my own two feet. When sickness threatens the lives of those I love, I am brought to my knees in grief. Still, you are the God of the afflicted. You are the Lord of every victim. You are the helper of the fatherless. You take us in hand, and you comfort us.

Comfort me, God, in times of great sorrow. Hold me together when I feel my life is falling apart. I have known you as the God of my great joy; I want to know you as the God of my great consolation and support.

I declare that no matter how alone I feel in my life, there is one who sees. There is one who knows the depths of my trauma, and he calls me his child. He is my comfort, my strength, and my relief. My God will never abandon me, no matter who else may leave my side.

Hold On

Let us hold firmly to the hope that we have confessed,
because we can trust God to do what he promised.

HEBREWS 10:23 NCV

Glorious God, I hold on to the hope that you awakened within my heart when I first knew you. I remember the awe I felt at your mysterious peace filling my soul. I recall the way I could not verbalize the gratitude I felt deep within my spirit. I will not forget the way my future seemed to stretch out in endless possibilities of your goodness with the knowledge that you were guiding me.

So, I hold on. I will not abandon the hope you planted, tended to, and ripened in your presence. I trust that you will continue to be faithful to your Word and that you will do all you have promised to do.

I declare that I am firmly rooted and established in the love of God. I will not be torn from the kingdom of my God who called me his own and set me free. With the Lord as my help and my constant companion, I hold on to the hope of a bright future and a beautiful present.

Gladness

The hope of the righteous ends in gladness,
but the expectation of the wicked comes to nothing.

PROVERBS 10:28 NRSV

Great God, I know that with my hopes rooted in you, I will not be disappointed. You continue to work out your faithfulness in the world, and my life is no exception. I trust that you will do exceedingly more than I can even think to imagine in your graciousness.

I must redirect my focus and expectations from things that are temporal and ever-changing to you. You never shift or change, and your character is immaculate and immovable. I love how wonderful you are! I fix my eyes on you, Lord, the author and perfector of my faith.

I declare that my hope is in Jesus and not in what I will gain or achieve in this world. Accolades and celebrity are of no value to me. I live with integrity, kindness, and mercy as my guiding values. I will experience the gladness of God's kingdom in fullness, and until that day, I will see glorious glimpses of it.

Every Detail Matters

"Don't worry. For your Father cares deeply
about even the smallest detail of your life."

MATTHEW 10:30-31 TPT

Father, thank you for not simply caring about the big
things in life. You also tend to the details. You care for the
birds of the air, the fish of the sea, and the creatures of the
dirt. You do not despise even the smallest longing. What I
see as insignificant, you value.

May I never underestimate the power and breadth of your
mercy. It meets every creature and takes care of every
detail. I trust you with the littlest things in my life as well as
the largest. Give me eyes to see where you are working on
the minutiae of my day-to-day.

*I declare that worry is a waste of my energy, for God takes
care of the things I can't control. I now shift the focus of
anxious energy to the areas where I can move ahead in
practical ways. I let go of the need to know how every
detail will work out. I trust that it will come together in
God's mercy.*

Recognition

"Whoever acknowledges me before others,
I will also acknowledge before my Father in heaven."

MATTHEW 10:32 NIV

Jesus, I yield my life to you. The fullness I am looking for is with you. You have led me to the Father through arms of open-hearted love and the power of your mercy. You take my weakness, and you make me strong. I offer you my heart, and you flood it with your peace that passes all understanding. You have purified me by the power of your love, and I stand clean before you.

How could I not sing your praises? There is no one better to me than you, and there never will be. I worship you with my life.

I am cleansed by the blood of the Lamb, and I stand in confidence before the throne of the Father. Jesus is my perfection, not my perfectionist pursuits. As I humble myself before him, he lifts me up. I am not ashamed of the power of the cross or the testimony of the overwhelming mercy of Jesus. I am free to live in his love, and I won't hide it.

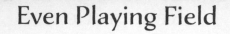

Even Playing Field

God does not show favoritism but accepts from every
nation the one who fears him and does what is right.

ACTS 10:34–35 NIV

Lord, I'm grateful that you don't play favorites. You love
each of us wholly and completely. There is no competition
in your love. I don't have to fight for your attention; I have
it whenever I turn to you.

I humble my heart before you today and ask for your
wisdom to guide me in my decisions. I love you more than
I can express. I am filled with gratitude for your immense
kindness in my life. Love me to life yet again in the purity of
your presence. I long for more than I have yet tasted, and I
want to walk in the integrity of your kingdom values.

*I am loved by God, and I am his child. I declare that my
identity is rooted and established in the limitlessness of
his mercy. No one can take from me what God has already
established. I will walk in the light of his ways with truth
and love guarding my heart.*

Remember

Do not throw away this confident trust in the Lord.
Remember the great reward it brings you!

HEBREWS 10:35 NLT

Faithful One, I don't want to turn away from you even when it is difficult to understand your ways. Keep me close to you in loyal love, Broaden my understanding with the perspective shift of your eternal point of view. I want to see what you see and know what you know.

I will continue to press into you with my questions and search for you in the messiness of this life. I believe that you are good; that goodness is coming. You are my greatest reward. Knowing you is my highest aim. Meet with me as I turn again to you.

As I remember what the Lord has promised, I am filled with confident hope in his faithfulness. He has not abandoned me, and he never changes. Instead of shifting with the winds of this world, I set my sails to catch the wind of his Spirit. I will not forget the benefits of trusting him.

Keep Persevering

You need to persevere so that when you have done the will of God, you will receive what he has promised.

HEBREWS 10:36 NIV

Constant One, fill my heart with your strength today. I am weak, and my attempts to follow you are rerouted by distractions. You are my compass. You are my guiding light. I will not stop trusting you to lead me along the path of your love. I will follow you. When I wander, I trust you to guide me back to your mercy.

I don't want to miss a single thing that you are doing. I don't want to miss a word that you are saying. You are my hope, and I cling to you. I won't stop coming back to you over and over again. In that place, I discover that you are already near and already at work.

As I continue to press into the present peace of God, I am filled with the courage I need to keep putting one foot in front of the other. His grace and strength become my own. I won't give up.

Open-hearted Belief

If you openly declare that Jesus is Lord and believe in your heart that God raised him from the dead, you will be saved. For it is by believing in your heart that you are made right with God, and it is by openly declaring your faith that you are saved.

ROMANS 10:9-10 NLT

Lord Jesus, I believe that you are the Son of God. I believe that you revealed the way to the Father and that he waits with open arms to welcome all who come to you. You are my Savior, and I trust in you.

Though the world may be full of ways to find acceptance, my deepest well of belonging is in your presence. I have never known a love like yours. You do not have hidden motives in your mercy. You transform me in the light of your presence, and I find I am free to be myself. I finally know what home feels like, and it is with you.

I am not ashamed of the gospel of Christ. It is my freedom, my joy, and my hope. I declare that as I live open-heartedly before God and others, the light of Jesus will shine through my life.

Every Generation

The LORD is good and his love endures forever;
his faithfulness continues through all generations.

PSALM 100:5 NIV

Lord, how wonderful is your unending love; how great is
your goodness toward me! I recognize your faithfulness
throughout the generations, and I am looking for it today.
From age to age, you have not changed in the slightest.
You are the same merciful God you have always been.

Open my understanding to see where you are working
mighty miracles of mercy in the world and in my life. I
will offer you thanks as I recognize each one. What you
have done for others, I believe you will also do for me.
Your character is unflinching in this world of shifting value
systems. I want to live according to your will and ways. You
are worthy of my praise.

*The Lord is good, and his love endures forever. He is
good to all he has made and that includes me. His love is
unending and that includes me. His faithfulness continues
through every single generation and yes, that includes mine.*

He Answers

He will answer the prayers of the needy;
he will not reject their prayers.

PSALM 102:17 NCV

Faithful Father, thank you for not only hearing my prayers but for answering them. As I wait on you, I know that you will renew my strength in your presence. Be the healer my heart and body so desperately need. Be the lifter of my head and give me the courage I need to face the unknowns that life brings.

I need you more than I need anything else. You are air I breathe, light to my eyes, and food that sustains me. I won't stop praying. I won't stop asking. I won't stop seeking you. Stoop down, Lord, and meet me in the midst of my current trials and troubles. Lift me up when I have no strength to stand on my own. Answer me, Lord!

Though I am needy, God my Father is abundant in all I require. He has not left me; he tends to my needs. If the birds of the air and the flowers of the field have no reason to worry, than neither do I. He will take care of me.

Look Up

As high as the heavens are above the earth,
so great is his steadfast love toward those who fear him.

PSALM 103:11 ESV

Great God, when I look at the mountains and see how the light dances off of them, I feel more connected to the present. When I watch the light of the sun filter through passing clouds, my heart swells with wonder. Though I can't begin to describe what the beauty of nature elicits within me, I know that I feel more connected to you through it all.

On a clear, starry night, I think of you. As high as those heavens that reach through galaxies, so great is your love. It is immeasurable, expansive, and breathtaking! Thank you.

The love of the Lord is as high as the reach of the heavens. As wide as the east is from the west, so is the mercy of God. There is no way to contain it, filter it, or reduce its breadth. This love is in constant movement toward me. I am met by love at every turn.

Fatherly Love

As a father shows compassion to his children,
so the Lord shows compassion to those who fear him.

Psalm 103:13 esv

Compassionate Father, I am grateful that you are not a distant, powerful leader who rules with an iron fist. You are a tender father who cares for his family. Thank you for bringing me into your family and for giving me your name. I am never without mercy because I am never without you.

As I come to you with all that's on my heart, meet me with your compassion. Instruct me, advise me, and speak truth over my heart. I want to know you more. As I do, I will reflect your likeness in my life. May the values of your kingdom become my values. I love you!

God is a loving father, a loyal friend, and a merciful judge. He shows compassion to those who honor him. I am revived by him every time he meets me with the fullness of his Spirit. I will show that same love and compassion to those around me.

Wonderful God

Praise the LORD, my soul, and forget not all his benefits—
who forgives all your sins and heals all your diseases.

PSALM 103:2-3 NIV

Lord, I will not forget how wonderful you are. Today I think
about the wonders of your character and how your power
has transformed the lives of others as well as my own.
There isn't a single confession I have made to you that has
caused you to turn away or reject me.

Thank you for forgiving my selfish choices, for making right
the wrongs that I have made, and for giving me courage
to walk in the light of your ways. You are my healer, my
restorer, and my Redeemer. I praise you for all you have
done and for who you are.

*I have been forgiven, redeemed, and set free to live in the
light of God's love. Today I live with gratitude on my lips and
purpose within my heart to know him more. I will not forget
his benefits. I will look for his goodness here and now.*

Crowned with Life

He redeems me from death
and crowns me with love and tender mercies.
He fills my life with good things.
My life is renewed like the eagle's!

PSALM 103:4-5 NLT

Redeemer, you are the best thing in my life. You renew and refresh me in your presence. You give me strength in my weakness. You redeem me from the curse of death and crown me with your love and tender kindness.

For all the mercy you have shown me, you're still not finished pouring out your love. You revive my heart when its faith wanes. Your present goodness reminds me that your faithfulness will never diminish. You are good, and your love endures forever and ever.

I have been redeemed by the love of Christ. I am a new creation in him, and my past does not define my future. He is my living hope, my holy pursuit, and my greatest reward. As I go about my day, his love goes with me. Thank you, Lord!

Overwhelming Love

The LORD is compassionate and gracious,
slow to anger, abounding in love.

PSALM 103:8 NIV

Gracious God, I have never known someone so patient and kind. You are slow to anger and rich in loyal love. You never withhold your mercy from those who look for you. You are not hard to find; you are easy to discover and to please.

I give you my attention today. I want to know the lengths of your love. I want to be aware with all my senses how deep, how wide, how high, and how long your mercy goes. Reveal the glory of your presence to me. I need you! You are my sustenance, my source, and my strength. You nurture me, and I develop in your care.

I have no reason to hide from my Maker. There is more than enough grace, limitless compassion, and unending mercy ready to meet me. He knows me through and through, so I will come to him with open arms and an unrestrained heart.

Liberator

He brought them out of darkness
and the shadow of death,
and broke their chains in pieces.

PSALM 107:14 NKJV

Jesus, you are my freedom fighter. You are the liberator who opens prison doors and breaks the shackles off our limbs. No shame can hold us down when your love liberates us from fear.

I want to walk in the light of your presence all the days of my life. I want to be so close to you that I can hear your whispers as clearly as I can hear the laughter of my loved ones. There is no one else like you, my liberator and my joy. I will not wallow in the shadows, waiting for you to pass by. Even in the darkest valley, you are with me, and I know you will lead me out of the clutches of my trials. You are good!

I declare that no matter what has tried to keep me stuck in this life, it has no power over my destiny. I am free in the love of Christ—free to live, move, and have my being. I am free to run in the fields of his goodness. I am free indeed.

Soul Satisfaction

He satisfies the longing soul,
and the hungry soul he fills with good things.

PSALM 107:9 ESV

Lord, you satisfy the deep longings of my soul. I believe that you will continue to do so. Where I feel longing, meet me with the purity of your presence. Where I am waiting, encourage me with your promises. Fill me with the confidence of your love and feed me with the goodness of your character.

You are faithful, and you will continue to be. I believe that I will see your goodness in my life more and more as I learn to ground myself in the gratitude of what is here now. You are with me, and you are more than enough for everything I face.

My soul finds its satisfaction in God alone. Though I may have dreams that come true and others that dissolve, the presence of God is full of lasting joy, peace, and love. I will cultivate a heart of gratitude for what I already have and for Christ. He is for me and in me.

Quiet Confidence

My heart, O God, is quiet and confident,
all because of you.
Now I can sing my song with passionate praises!
Awake, O my soul, with the music of his splendor.

PSALM 108:1 TPT

O God, awaken my soul in the light of your goodness. As the sun rises and brings hope for a new day, will you rise over me and clear the cobwebs of doubt? You are my confidence. There is nothing greater I could attain to in this life than to know you and to walk in open fellowship with you.

You have come through for me before, and I know you will do it again. I will sing passionate praises as I did before. But even here in the waiting, I will sing your praise, for you are worthy and good.

My confidence is in the Lord and his unchanging nature. His faithfulness will never relent. He will not shift his mind from loyal love. Even when I feel doubt, his faithfulness shines through like the sun breaking through the clouds. I declare that my heart will trust him implicitly.

Confident Assurance

Faith is confidence in what we hope for
and assurance about what we do not see.

HEBREWS 11:1 NIV

Faithful One, thank you for your faithfulness that is not dependent upon my faith. Still, you honor the faith of those who look to you. I am confident that all my hopes, rooted in your unchanging nature, will be fulfilled. You will not forget a promise you have made or a word you have spoken. You are not flippant, and you are not untrustworthy. You are more faithful than the most loyal person that has ever walked this earth.

You are better than the best of us. I believe that you are continuing to work your mercy in my life and in the world. You are wonderful!

God is not a man that he would lie. He is not fickle that he would change his mind. Confident assurance is our response of faith to a God who transcends time and space, who lovingly reaches us where we are, and who never fails.

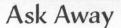

Ask Away

"I tell you, whatever you ask in prayer,
believe that you have received it,
and it will be yours."

MARK 11:24 ESV

Good God, I lay out my heart like an open book before you today. I bring you all my questions, longings, and hopes. I ask for that which I have kept to myself for fear of sounding selfish or silly. I am grateful that your love for me knows no bounds. You do not demean what I value, and yet your wisdom transcends my own understanding.

I yield my life to you, God. As I pray with openness and trust today, I choose to believe that you will honor my prayers because you are a good father. I want to know you, Lord. Instruct me in your wisdom even as I ask for what is on my heart.

I can come to the King of kings with confidence because I am his beloved child. I can ask without hemming or hawing because he knows me and delights in me. I have no reason to hide and no reason to question his love. I am confident of this: the one that I pray to is incomparably good, righteous, and faithful.

The Way

"I am the resurrection and the life. The one who believes in me will live, even though they die; and whoever lives by believing in me will never die."

JOHN 11:25-26 NIV

Lord Jesus, I have found true freedom through you. Your resurrection power is the power that liberates me and has ushered me into your kingdom. Though I have seen glimpses of your glorious goodness in this life, I know that fullness is coming.

Your life in mine has expanded my ability to be present and full of peace, joy, love, hope, and compassion in ways that I could never anticipate. Even though my body will surely fail me, you never will. You are my living hope, and that hope will never die.

In the resurrection life of Jesus, I come alive. I declare that there is no fear of death, pain, sickness, or loss that can ever separate me from the overcoming love of Christ. I am fully alive in him, and I will always be.

Real Rest

"Come to me, all you who are weary and burdened, and I will give you rest."

MATTHEW 11:28 NIV

Good Shepherd, I find rest in your presence whenever I need it. Today I need it! Refresh me with your living waters of love and lift the burdens that weigh me down. I can't bear the load of worries and anxiety that have slowly chipped away at my strength.

Transform me with your peace and restore my soul. I partner with you, and I know you do all the heavy lifting. Minister to my heart and calm my mind as I rest in you right now. I breathe in your love and your peace. Spirit, move again in me.

I declare that my strength is not found in the weight of what I carry on my own; it is found in the partnership of Christ. I will rest in his presence and lean into the confidence of his faithfulness. I find true and lasting peace here.

Greatest Teacher

"Take my yoke upon you and learn from me,
for I am gentle and humble in heart,
and you will find rest for your souls."

MATTHEW 11:29 NIV

Jesus, you are humbler and gentler than all and yet more powerful than everyone. You are the living expression of the Father, and there is nothing you can't do. You chose to humble yourself as a servant to all. You healed the sick, took time with the outcasts, and had dinner with those the religious elite shunned. You did not turn anyone away who came to you. You do the same today. You welcome those who open their hearts and homes to you.

I want to learn from you, Jesus, and walk in your ways. May I become gentler and humbler as I know you more. May rhythms of rest keep me fueled for the work that is mine to do.

I declare that Jesus is my greatest teacher. I look to him for wisdom, instruction, and direction to live out his love in my life. I will find rest in him even as he leads me through the hilltops and valleys of this life.

March

We are confident that he
hears us whenever we ask for
anything that pleases him.

1 John 5:14 NLT

More than Meets the Eye

It is by faith we understand that the whole world was made by God's command so what we see was made by something that cannot be seen.

HEBREWS 11:3 NCV

Creator, though I did not see you create the universe, I believe that it is from your hand. Just as I believe that you created the world and declared it good, I also believe that you created me with purpose. Your love knows no bounds, and it encompasses everything I can see and so much more.

Increase my faith in your faithfulness as you continue to move in my life and in the earth. Root my heart in the soil of your mercy, the source of every nutrient I need to grow and flourish. I rely on you, Lord. I believe that you are doing much more under the surface of what I know. I believe that you will continue to move in goodness, righteousness, and mercy.

I do not need to understand the intricacies of God's ways to know his heart. I am firmly rooted and established in his love, and there my faith is nourished. I will grow even more confident in his mercy as I live with a heart yielded to his kingdom ways.

Come to Him

Without faith living within us it would be impossible to please God. For we come to God in faith knowing that he is real and that he rewards the faith of those who give all their passion and strength into seeking him.

HEBREWS 11:6 TPT

Lord, I come to you with a heart full of questions as well as a heart full of faith. I believe that you are not afraid of my curiosity. I will find wisdom in your leadership. You do not require blind obedience; you want a heart open and willing to trust you.

I do trust you! I come to you with all that is churning in my soul, and I lay it out before you. Thank you for the freedom to be open with you about everything. Fill me with the comfort of your present peace and the clarity of your unmatched wisdom as I submit my thoughts to you today. I direct my passion and strength toward you, for you are the source of all things.

I declare that the seeds of faith in my heart have been planted by God himself. I do not need to ignore any part of me but rather present my whole self completely to him. He is good, and he will not turn me away.

Unoffended

"Blessed is anyone who takes no offense at me."

MATTHEW 11:6 NRSV

Jesus, there is so much in this world that causes my hackles to rise and defend my biases. You, though, are unoffendable. Thank you for your mercy that reaches everyone in the same measure. You do not withhold your love from anyone willing to receive it. Though my pride may want to conceal where I have bought into false narratives of who you are, I choose to humble myself before you.

Wash over my mind with your clarity and breathe the expanse of your peace into my soul. Give me eyes to see from your perfect perspective. I lay down my own righteous excuses in favor of your pure compassion. I want to live as you did, Jesus, yielded to the Father's heart. I choose to follow you on the path of your loyal love.

I am not ashamed of Jesus, and I will not let the challenge of his love keep me from following his ways. His ways are better, truer, and purer than the ways of mankind. I choose to walk in the kingdom ways of Jesus and to follow his example.

Trustworthy and True

All he does is just and good,
and all his commandments are trustworthy.

PSALM 111:7 NLT

Almighty God, I believe that you are just, kind, and good. All you do is rooted in the perfection of your loving character. You do not judge us harshly, and you don't ever go back on your Word. You are full of truth, and you always will be.

Guide me, Spirit, and lead me to the rock that is greater than I. I build my life upon the solid foundation of your nature. When storms blow in, my foundation will not be shaken. When wars break out, the solid rock of your love will not move from my life. You are the source of everything good in my life. You are the one who decides when to give and when to withhold. I trust you.

I declare that all goodness in my life is from the Lord. He has not forgotten a single promise he has spoken. He will faithfully fulfill everything he has set out to do, and I don't need to worry about it.

Light of Mercy

A light shines in the dark for honest people,
for those who are merciful and kind and good.

PSALM 112:4 NCV

Jesus, as I spend time with you, I know that your wisdom
will not leave me unaffected. I want to become more and
more like you. You, who are limitlessly merciful, kind, and
good, are the one I pledge my life to. Teach me to walk in
the ways of your gracious love. I will choose honesty over
deceit, compassion over judgment, and promoting peace
over proving my point.

You are so much better than I could dream of being, and
yet your Spirit at work within me transforms me into your
image. I'm so grateful to know you and to be known by
you. The radiance of your light shines on my life and brings
hope, joy, and fulfillment.

*I am made in the image of love itself, and I become
more like God as I behold the wonderful nature of Jesus.
As I fellowship with God, my life is transformed by his
friendship. There is no greater aim than to know him and to
be known by him.*

Return to Rest

Return to your rest, my soul,
for the Lord has been good to you.

PSALM 116:7 NIV

Loving Lord, I am grateful that I can find true rest, right here and now, in your presence. Spirit, surround me with your peace as I turn my attention toward you. I recount the ways in which your goodness has met me this week, month, and year. I recall the kindnesses of your mercy that have been so clearly sown into my story. I see the fruit of your love at work in my life, and it is with gratitude that I give you my adoration and praise today.

Lead my soul to real rest as I dwell on you. Do more than calm my mind; expand my soul with your spacious love. Reach into the recesses of my soul and water the seeds of your kingdom within me with your living waters.

I declare that my soul finds rest in God alone. There is no better source of peace than the Spirit of God alive within me. There is no purer spring of joy than the joy of the Lord. I am refreshed and revived in his presence.

Great Kindness

His merciful kindness is great toward us,
And the truth of the Lᴏʀᴅ endures forever.
Praise the Lᴏʀᴅ!

Psᴀʟᴍ 117:2 ɴᴋᴊᴠ

Merciful Lord, I am undone by your great kindness toward me. The way you love me so tenderly while never changing your perfect nature is hard to comprehend. Still, your love transforms me continually and increases the passion of my heart for you.

You propel me to be more compassionate with others, to offer mercy instead of judgment, and to stand for justice rather than sitting in apathy. Your truth stands firm forever, and I know you will never change. May I reflect your kindness in my life so that your love shines brightly.

I will praise the Lord with my actions, not just my mouth. I choose to live with love as my highest value. I align myself with the kingdom values of Jesus, and I humble myself before him. I declare that my heart is yielded to his, and I am not indifferent to his words of wisdom. I can freely give compassion to others because I have been offered compassion freely.

Higher Trust

It is better to take refuge in the LORD
than to trust in people.

PSALM 118:8 NLT

Lord, though I am prone to look for security in the world around me, I know that true security is found in you. There are no guarantees in this life. I don't want to build my life upon something and wake up to find that the foundation has cracked and was faulty from the start. I want to be found firmly planted upon your nature.

You will never abandon your promises, and you won't ever stop being merciful. Build me up from the inside out with the power of your love. I can trust you implicitly. You are my refuge, and I run into the shelter of your presence.

I declare that my safest space is in the shelter of the Lord. His presence is my refuge, and I am covered by his love all the days of my life. I will not trust the words of others more than I do his Word. His truth will stand firm throughout the ages.

Source of Hope

You are my refuge and my shield;
your word is my source of hope.

PSALM 119:114 NLT

Lord, you are a shield around me when fiery darts of accusation fly my way. When lies are spreading and my character is brought into question without the basis of truth, I run to you. Defender, take up my cause. Protect me from slander and don't let lies destroy me.

I will not add fuel to the fire of others' indignation when their contempt has blinded them. I will not do the emotional labor of trying to convince those who are only seeing red. I trust you to reveal what is right and to keep me at rest in your perfect peace. I trust you to defend me. You are my hope, and I rely on you.

I do not need to defend myself against the accusations of those who do not know me or anything about me. I do not need to throw punches at the air; I can trust the Lord to reveal the truth. I trust him to do what I can't, and I will reserve my energy for the things that matter.

Ever So Near

You are near, O LORD,
and all your commands are true.

PSALM 119:151 NLT

Lord, be near. Your Word says that you are close. Your Spirit is a comforter, not just by the words that are spoken but by the felt nearness of love incarnate. Your peace is present and not just an ideology. Your joy is not wishful thinking; it's a real sense of your abiding pleasure.

I open my heart to you and turn my attention toward you. I offer you the space and time to speak into me your words of life. I welcome your presence to surround and fill me. I long to know you more with not just with my intellect but also with my very being and life. I want to experience your nearness with all my senses. Come close, Lord, and do not delay.

The Spirit of the Lord is upon me, for I have yielded my life to him. He comes with power, not simply words. He is my source of joy, strength, peace, comfort, hope, and love. He is near.

Justice Reigns

The very essence of your words is truth;
all your just regulations will stand forever.

PSALM 119:160 NLT

God of Justice, you do not turn a blind eye to evil intent, and you don't write off those who seek to destroy others. You are merciful in all you do, and yet you are also fully just. I trust you to uphold justice in ways that humankind can never get right.

I will not be apathetic about causes that need voices to speak for them, but I will also not base all my hopes on the governments of this world. They are imperfect, and they always will be no matter who is in power. I'm so grateful that you hold more power than the people of this world. You are just, you are full of truth, and you are compassionate. You are the best judge, and I will not take your place in the court of opinion.

I declare that God's justice is purer than my own. Though I think I know best, God knows so much better. I will trust him with this role even as I partner with him to see justice come to earth in greater measure.

Great Peace

Those who love your instructions
have great peace and do not stumble.

Psalm 119:165 nlt

Prince of Peace, I find greatest clarity in your wisdom. I
find rest in your truth. Your guidance is full of loyal love,
giving freedom of choice and advising me with your higher
perspective. I don't need to worry about getting it wrong
when love is my motivation. I don't have to fear failure
because your grace is big enough to cover and redeem
any mistakes I make. There is freedom to walk in the
fullness of your mercy because you surround me with your
faithfulness.

I will never be perfect, but you don't require my perfection.
What liberation I have found in this truth! Though life
will bring trials and tests of my character, your love will
never waver, and your peace will not be upset. I love your
wisdom, and I walk in your ways.

*I have the peace of God as my portion today. I have the
plentiful peace of God as my forever portion. I do not need
to fear the unknown with Jesus as my guide. His wisdom
will instruct, redirect, and heal me. I trust him.*

Preserved by Promise

My comfort in my suffering is this:
your promise preserves my life.

PSALM 119:50 NIV

God, I find tremendous comfort in your faithfulness. Your promises spoken over me preserve my life. I will remember what you have said, and I will cling to your Word in faith. You are better than the kindest father, more devoted than the most loyal lover, and more tender than a caring mother. I trust you to do everything you have set out to do in my life.

Even when I walk through the valley of the shadow of death, I won't be afraid. You are with me. You will uphold me, strengthen me, and rejuvenate me. When my flesh fails, you are still faithful.

I declare that God's promises endure forever. No one can convince him out of them. I am safe and secure in the faithfulness of God, no matter the troubles I walk through or the suffering I endure. He is not finished with me yet.

Let Wisdom Lead

Wise words bring many benefits,
and hard work brings rewards.

PROVERBS 12:14 NLT

Yahweh, I look to you today. Instruct me with your unparalleled wisdom and encourage my heart in your faithfulness. I don't want shortcuts or quick fixes; I want what lasts. When I am hasty to move ahead, slow me down with your counsel. I want to learn to enjoy the present as much as the prospects of the future. Help me to sink into the moment and dig in with tenacity and perseverance where you have put me.

I know that there is work to do here where my feet are planted, and I won't waste time dreaming away the moment I have at hand. Wisdom, strengthen my soul with your counsel and make firm my resolve.

I declare that this is the day the Lord has made, so I will do what is mine to do here and now. I won't wish away the gift of the present moment, and I won't waste what is already mine to cultivate. I dig into my field and press into his presence as I heed his wisdom.

Many Parts

If the whole body were an eye, it would not be able to hear. If the whole body were an ear, it would not be able to smell. If each part of the body were the same part, there would be no body. But truly God put all the parts, each one of them, in the body as he wanted them.

1 CORINTHIANS 12:17-18 NCV

Father, I find my true self in you. You have created me, with all my quirks and tendencies, just as you wanted me. You gave me the talents that I possess, and I get to partner with your creativity in cultivating them.

Thank you for the gifts you placed in me with purpose. I want to truly embody the gift it is to be me. I don't want to wish my one life away by wasting time comparing where I am with where others are. Give me insight into the gifts that you have placed within me; I want to tend to them and develop them with your wisdom and leadership. Thank you for the freedom I have to be fully me, for your liberating love is alive within me.

I am God's handiwork, and I am made in his image. I declare that my life has purpose and meaning, and I will not try to conform to others' ideas any longer. My true identity is found in God and in whom I am wholly and divinely loved.

Divine Pioneer

Looking to Jesus the pioneer and perfecter of our faith, who for the sake of the joy that was set before him endured the cross, disregarding its shame, and has taken his seat at the right hand of the throne of God.

HEBREWS 12:2 NRSV

Jesus, you are the pioneer of perfect love. There is no one more qualified to speak on God's behalf. You are the living expression of mercy. You are one with Father and Spirit, and you show us the way to come home to him. You did not consider the shame, humiliation, and pain you would face as more important than us knowing the incredible resurrection power of God's mercy.

I want to follow you on the pathway of your love. You are alive, and you are with the Father. I count the cost of choosing your ways, and I follow you.

I declare that my life belongs to Jesus. I want to reflect the same love of the Father that Jesus Christ revealed to those who would listen and see. I have eyes to see and ears to hear what he is saying.

No Other

Behold, God is my salvation,
I will trust and not be afraid;
For the LORD God is my strength and my song,
And He has become my salvation.

ISAIAH 12:2 NASB

Savior, you are my God, and you are my rescuer. I will trust you more than I trust myself. I will depend on you more than I depend on those around me. I will not be afraid, for you are with me. Even now, as I am reading these words, you are present.

You have not forgotten what you spoke over me, and you will not abandon your Word. You are my strength and my song. You are my salvation and my only hope. Your living love awakens me from the slumber of my anxiety, and you clear the fog of my confusion. You are the light of my life; shine on me once more.

I am redeemed and restored in the overwhelming mercy of God. He is my hope, my salvation, and my very life source. He is all I need, and I will not fear the unknowns of tomorrow. Right now, God is with me. Right now, I have everything I need.

Never Abandoned

The LORD will not abandon His people on account of
His great name, because the LORD has been pleased to
make you a people for Himself.

1 SAMUEL 12:22 NASB

Lord, your faithfulness works in accordance with your
character. Your unfailing love does not waver or recede.
You are full of pure passion for your people, and that will
never change.

Transform my heart as I meditate on your exceeding
goodness. The promise of your nearness, your constant
support, and your unending mercy is more than I can
comprehend. Thank you for never abandoning me. You do
not leave your people, and you don't walk away from those
who look to you. Thank you!

*I am a part of God's family, and he will never abandon his
children. I am firmly established in his kingdom, for he is
my entry point and my eternal salvation. I will not fear, no
matter what today brings, for God is with me. He won't
leave my side.*

Unshakeable Kingdom

Since we are receiving a kingdom that cannot be shaken, let us be thankful, and so worship God acceptably with reverence and awe.

HEBREWS 12:28 NIV

God, I worship you today. I am in awe of how consistently you move in goodness and mercy. There is no chain that you can't break, no dilemma that you can't turn around, and no wound that you can't heal. You are so much better than I could ever give you credit for.

Thank you for the unending hope I have in your unfailing kingdom that is sure to come in fullness. The foundation of your righteousness can't be moved. The capstone of your mercy can't be shaken.

I am full of gratitude for the unwavering promise of God's kingdom. There will come a day when every pain, every loss, and every injustice is set right. The Lord is good, his love endures forever, and I am covered in the abundance of his mercy even as I wait for the fullness of his leadership.

Deep Joy

With joy you will drink deeply
from the fountain of salvation.

PSALM 12:3 NLT

Savior, it is with deep joy that I drink from the fountain of
your present help. It is with reverence that I look to you
today. You are my holy hope, my saving grace, and the
source of all I long for in this life. Your promises are true,
and you never stop working your faithfulness in this world.

Though I may let myself and others down, you never do.
You are not like us that you would change your mind with
passing trends. You are the way, the truth, and the life. You
are full of delight and pleasure. I find deeper delight in your
liberating love than I could ever imagine. Thank you for
calling me you own; I am so grateful to be yours.

*My joy is found in the presence of the Lord, and therefore I
have deep joy available to me today! No matter what I face,
the joy of the Lord is my strength.*

Don't Worry

"People everywhere seem to worry about making a living, but your heavenly Father knows your every need and will take care of you."

LUKE 12:30 TPT

Father, you know how quick I am to worry about the future when my ideals are upset, or unknowns break through the cracks of my life. I know that you are not surprised by anything. Though a multitude of disruptions and distractions keep my focus shifting, you see everything with perfect clarity.

I rely on your heavenly wisdom to guide me in my decisions and to calm my anxious heart when I lose control. I trust that you will continue to guide me into your goodness and never leave me along the way. You know my needs, and I trust you to take care of me.

I am a child of the living God, and he will take care of me. When troubles arise and I lose my focus, God is unshaken. He sees the end to the beginning and everything in between. He takes care of what I could never anticipate, so I will trust him above myself and all others.

Same God

God works in different ways,
but it is the same God who does the work in all of us.

1 Corinthians 12:6 NLT

Loving Lord, I'm so grateful that you are a creative being. You did not make humans to be carbon copies of each other. The whole earth tells the story of your creativity. The mountains and the plains are so different, yet they are your handiwork. The animals of the jungles and the creatures of the sea are your creation.

There are such different climates, cultures, and traditions in this world, but you don't belong to one of them. You are in them all, bringing light to shadows and wonder to open eyes. My understanding is expanded as I consider how endlessly imaginative and inventive you are.

Though God moves in many different ways, his character is the same through it all. The fruit of his Spirit is consistent in everything he does. I will not put him in a box of my own making, and I will not diminish him to fit my understanding.

Generous Grace

He said to me, "My grace is sufficient for you, for my power is made perfect in weakness." Therefore I will boast all the more gladly about my weaknesses, so that Christ's power may rest on me.

2 Corinthians 12:9 niv

Gracious God, in my weakness, pour the power of your grace into me. Your infinite resource of mercy is the fuel that sustains me. I rely on you when I have nothing else to cling to.

When everything is going well in life, it can be easy to think that I've earned my peace. Still, I know that your perfect peace is present no matter the pain I may experience. All I have is from you, and all I need is found in you. I look to you today, no matter how strong or how weak I feel. Move in power in my life.

No matter how well or how horribly my day is going, God's abundant grace is my source of strength. With his power at work in me, I will experience his resurrection life.

Love and Peace

Be joyful. Grow to maturity. Encourage each other. Live in harmony and peace. Then the God of love and peace will be with you.

2 Corinthians 13:11 NLT

Prince of Peace, I'm so grateful that your love cultivates growth and is never stagnant. With my roots planted in your loyal mercy, I find joy is a deep well within me where your Spirit lives. I find that I am growing in wisdom and maturity as I look to you and live out your kingdom ways. I find encouragement breeds inspiration, and I will not hold it back from anyone.

As I promote peace and seek to live in harmony, I choose the path of love rather than my own comfort. Your ways are expansive, and you are constantly drawing me out of my little life into the greater area of your kingdom where there is no end to your love, mercy, and truth. You set me free rather than hold me back, and I am forever grateful.

I am full of the loyal love of God that nourishes, strengthens, and expands my soul. My capacity for mercy grows as I practice encouraging others and seeing from the eyes of compassion rather than offense. I am fully loved, and I give from a place of overflow.

Things That Last

Three things will last forever—faith, hope, and love—
and the greatest of these is love.

1 CORINTHIANS 13:13 NLT

Faithful One, expand my understanding of the lengths of
your love, the limitlessness of your hope, and the power of
faith. You never stop weaving mercy into the fabric of our
lives. You don't turn away those who come to you.

May I be full of faith, overflowing in hope, and completely
submerged in love all the days of my life. If these are what
remain, I want them to be my guiding values. Let my life,
my choices, and my relationships reflect these values
of your kingdom, and may I be a shining light of your
powerful mercy that never gives up.

*Faith, hope, and love will never disappear, and they won't
lose their power. Today as I look to the Lord, I will be met
with an overabundance of these kingdom values. I am full
of faith, hope, and love.*

Impressionable

Spend time with the wise and you will become wise.
but the friends of fools will suffer.

PROVERBS 13:20 NCV

Spirit, you are the one I look to for wisdom above every other. In your truth, my confusion is set straight. The chaos of anxiety finds rest in your peace. The worries about tomorrow's unknowns are calmed with the steady strength of your faithfulness.

May I spend time with those who are wise and walking on the path of your pure love. May I know people who do not throw stones but offer relief to those who are suffering. Fools only care about their own lives and preferences, and I do not want to live a small, apathetic life. Wisdom, lead me home to you, and I will find the well of my own intuition there. I know that you will never lead me astray.

I will spend time with those who encourage me to live more selflessly and more compassionately. I will find people who challenge me to be my best self. I get to choose my company and community, and it is an act of wisdom to do so.

Rewarded Righteousness

Trouble pursues the sinner,
but the righteous are rewarded with good things.

PROVERBS 13:21 NIV

Lord, I align my life with your kingdom ways, not with the self-promoting ways of this world. I will not hide in the shadows. I will not live according to what others say is best for me but according to what you say I need. I will walk forward in faith, always stretching out in love, compassion, and kindness. I will not let the burden of people-pleasing keep me from living the fullness of my freedom in you.

I have been set free by your love, and I will live as a reflection of your wonderful mercy. I don't want to stay stuck in cycles of shame and trauma; I want to live in the expanse of your peace. You are my great reward, so I will keep following you.

Christ is my righteousness, so I do not have to rely on the merit of my own good deeds. He is my perfection, and I have been purified in his presence. There is nothing that he holds against me, so I will not hold myself to impossible and perfectionistic standards anymore. His mercy sets me free time and again.

Satisfied in the Moment

Don't love money; be satisfied with what you have.
For God has said, "I will never fail you.
I will never abandon you."

HEBREWS 13:5 NLT

Good Father, though I have plans for my future, only you know what it will be. I trust your ways more than I trust my own ideas of success. Though I'm grateful for resources, I will not put them above you. Though I am a creature of comfort, I will not allow my comfort to be my motivation in life.

I don't want to preserve myself or build a life that is filled with things but empty of meaning. I want to live a bigger life than I can build for myself. I want to live with love as my motivation and with a big, generous heart. I am grateful for what I have here and now. Help me to be satisfied and to look for ways to celebrate your gifts in my life. I know that you never fail. You won't abandon me.

I declare that I have all I need here in this moment. I do not need to race into the future because I can rest in the abundance I have right now. Each day will take care of itself, and God will not fail. My soul finds peace in this truth.

Forever the Same

Jesus Christ is the same
yesterday, today, and forever.

HEBREWS 13:8 NKJV

Jesus, when I look at your ministry and what you gave
your time, attention, and energy to, I can't help but be
astonished. You are as full of loyal mercy and kindness
today as you were in your earthly life. You did not turn
away from the needy, and you didn't ignore the vulnerable.
You still are a healer, a helper, and a pure example of the
living love of God the Father.

Thank you for the freedom I have found in your love. Thank
you for the walls that your mercy has torn down in my
heart. You are so much better than the rulers of this world,
and I give you my full allegiance.

*Jesus Christ is the same gracious, humble, loving,
challenging, hopeful, and healing God that he has always
been. I am covered in his mercy today, and I am met with
his compassion. This is true every day.*

Work It Out

The LORD will work out his plans for my life—
for your faithful love, O LORD, endures forever.
Don't abandon me, for you made me.

PSALM 138:8 NLT

O Lord, thank you for your faithful love that sustains me.
I trust you to work out your plans for my life. I give up
striving and worrying about what I can't control, and I
rest in your faithfulness. I don't have to stress about the
unknowns when you are the orchestrator of my story.

Even as I partner with you in my daily choices, I trust you
to do what I can't do. You are my creator, and I rest in the
confidence of your love. You are not surprised by anything
I do, and I know that even when I make mistakes, your
mercy turns my messes into gardens of your faithfulness.
You will never change, and that brings me great peace.

*I declare that I will do what I know to do, and I will leave
the rest in God's hands. I will not worry about the future,
for I have the companionship of God at every twist and turn
in my road.*

Even Greater

"I tell you the truth, anyone who believes in me will do the same works I have done, and even greater works, because I am going to be with the Father."

JOHN 14:12 NLT

Lord Jesus, you have shown me the way to be like you. You have revealed what the Father is like, and you have laid out what I should align myself with in life. Your call to compassion and your standard of mercy is unlike any other leader I have known. You are perfect in love and do not excuse any type of apathy or act of hatred in the name of God. You reveal that God is a patient and generous father, not hasty to judge and quick to restore when we turn to him.

I believe that your ways are better than the tendencies of humanity. I believe that as I align my life with yours and I look for ways to live out your love in this world, the fruit of your Spirit will powerfully work through my life. I long to know you more, reflect you more, and live as a shining beacon of your goodness.

Because I am a follower of Jesus, everything he did in his ministry is available to me through his Spirit. As I move in love and faith, he will work through me for the sake of his glory.

April

"You will call on me
and come and pray to me,
and I will listen to you."

JEREMIAH 29:12 NIV

For the Glory

> "Whatever you ask in my name, this I will do,
> that the Father may be glorified in the Son."
>
> JOHN 14:13 ESV

Glorious God, you are so generous in love and so patient in mercy. I have asked for things in your name before, and I won't stop doing it now. Every morning is a new opportunity to experience deeper levels of your love. Every moment is a fresh chance to seek you.

I lay out my heart openly and freely before you; I know that you meet me with pleasure and delight. Shine the light of your compassion on my heart and lift the heavy burdens I offer you. May you be glorified in my life as I move in your liberty.

I declare that I will not hold back a single request from the Lord today. Every time I go to him, I am met with loving acceptance. I come alive in the delight of his heart, and my own heart is moved in worship as he speaks his words of life and truth over me. Everything happens for his glory and my good.

Stay Still

"The LORD will fight for you,
you have only to be still."

EXODUS 14:14 NIV

Lord, I trust you to fight the battles I can't. I don't want to rush to my own defense over accusations that are empty and based on lies. I trust you to come to my defense; I rely on your power to set the record straight. You know my heart better than any other. No matter what others say, they can't convince you of something that is untrue.

I choose to remain in your presence, resting in the faithfulness of your mercy. As I lean into you, pull me close to your heart that exudes peace and wraps around me with protection. Do what only you can do and keep me in perfect peace as you do it. I trust you, Lord.

I do not need to defend myself against the accusations of those who do not know me. I trust the Lord to fight for me, and I will rest in the sustaining peace of his presence.

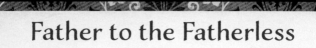

Father to the Fatherless

"No, I will not abandon you as orphans—
I will come to you."

JOHN 14:18 NLT

Faithful Father, you are so much better than anyone I have ever known. Though I have known love that is good, yours is purer than any other. You never misunderstand my intentions, and you don't misread my heart. You are more patient with me than I could imagine being with others. You never change. You do not abandon me, and your promise to be with me is unshakeable.

Your Spirit is my constant companion and help. You have come, and you will remain. I am more grateful to you than I could ever express.

God is a faithful father to the fatherless and to all whom others ignore. He never abandons those who have been discarded. He never sets me aside. He gathers me in, calls me his own, and promises to never leave or forsake me. What a friend. What a father. What a Savior!

There Is Room

"There are many rooms in my Father's house;
I would not tell you this if it were not true.
I am going there to prepare a place for you."

JOHN 14:2 NCV

Everlasting King, in a world where there are limitations everywhere we look, I am grateful that your kingdom is ever-expanding. Not only are there no limits to your love, but it is constantly moving in increasing measure. Though my mind can't comprehend this, my heart stirs. I am moved by the good news of your salvation, your welcome, and your heart toward me.

May my own love expand to see the possibilities of goodness, redemption, and hope around me. Your love can't be stopped by man-made measures. There are no boundaries that your love can't cross.

There is a place prepared for me in the kingdom of my God, and it is my place to take. There is room for everyone! I don't have to fight for my place at his table, and I don't need to push anyone away in order to belong. Love is expansive and inclusive; I will open my heart more to God's merciful kindness today.

Heavenly Teacher

"The Advocate, the Holy Spirit, whom the Father will send in my name, will teach you all things and will remind you of everything I have said to you."

JOHN 14:26 NIV

Holy Spirit, you are my teacher and my close confidant. Thank you for your presence with me. Thank you for the revelations you give of the Father's generous mercy. Thank you for dwelling with me in Spirit and in truth. I worship you just as I worship the Father and the Son.

Teach me the ways of the kingdom, and I will follow. Reveal the powerful wisdom of the truth, and I will walk in your ways. Thank you for your patience, gentleness, and generosity. Thank you for your comfort, clarity, and confidence. I depend on you more than I depend on any other. I trust your wisdom and revelation; I know they always hold the fruit of heaven.

I have a heavenly teacher available to me through the fellowship of the Spirit today. There is no problem too complicated, no confusion too cloudy, and no resistance too great that one revelation from the Spirit could not set straight. I lean into that wise voice today.

Secure Refuge

Those who fear the Lord are secure;
he will be a refuge for their children.

PROVERBS 14:26 NLT

Lord, I honor you as my Father, my leader, and my wise counselor. There is no one else who holds such words of life. There is no one else who is as faithfully true, loving, and powerful as you are. You are the refuge I run to when the troubles of this world are too much to bear. You are the safety I seek when the world is going crazy. I find peace and rest in your presence even when the battles of life are raging.

There is nothing that your mercy won't do. There are no lengths your love won't reach to cover your children. I am yours, Lord, and you are my safe place.

I choose to honor the Lord with my life and to worship him in spirit and in truth. He is my safe place, my refuge, and my peace. He keeps my heart at rest and takes the weight of my worries. He is faithful and true in all things, and I trust him.

Unrestricted Peace

"Peace I leave with you; my peace I give you.
I do not give to you as the world gives.
Do not let your hearts be troubled
and do not be afraid."

JOHN 14:27 NIV

Prince of Peace, I am so grateful that you don't give with condition. You give freely, fully, and without restraint. You offer the fullness of your mercy without a clause or hidden agenda. You are pure in peace, overwhelming in compassionate care, and outrageously abundant in tenderness. The authority of your love can never be thwarted. The power of your resurrection life can't be defeated, for it has already defeated the grave.

As my heart rests in your presence, I find my courage rises in the confidence of your faithfulness. I find rest in you. I won't let my heart get carried away by fear that pushes me to make hasty decisions not rooted in your love. I trust you.

I have the abundant peace of Christ as my portion today. He has already offered the fullness of his peace to those who look to him, so I will take him at his word. He does not move in empty promises but in the abundance of the Father's generosity.

Fountain of Life

The fear of the Lord is a fountain of life,
turning a person from the snares of death.

PROVERBS 14:27 NIV

Loving Lord, I know that as I yield my life continually to
your leadership, you will guide me in truth that refreshes
my soul and keeps me from the snares of foolishness. I
know that you are so much wiser than I am, and I submit
my decisions to you.

Your mercy is like a wide river carrying me through life. I
trust your guidance more than I do my own preferences.
The fruit of your Spirit assures me of your guidance, and
I know that you are a God who is faithful to his Word.
Lead me on through the dark valleys and on the craggy
mountaintops. I trust you today, and I trust you forever.

*I declare that with the Lord are the words of life and the
refreshing waters of his mercy. I choose to follow him today,
and I will listen to his wisdom that instructs me. I yield to
the Lord and his leadership.*

Coming Back

> "If I go and prepare a place for you,
> I will come back and take you to be with me
> that you also may be where I am."

Jesus, thank you for promising to return. I eagerly await the day when you will come back for those you love. In the meantime, build me up in your Spirit. Let your kingdom come and your will be done on earth as it is in heaven. Give me all I need for today: the necessities that will fuel my body, mind, and spirit.

Forgive me for the times I have ignored your wisdom. I long to be more like you. Help me to reach out in mercy and compassion to others just as you do with me. You are worthy of my time, my attention, and my submission.

I am not alone. I am covered, filled, and surrounded by the Spirit of Christ. With the Spirit as the seal of Jesus' promise, hope for his return dwells within my chest. I will live submitted to his love all the days of my life as I await his coming.

God of Peace

God is not a God of confusion
but a God of peace.

1 CORINTHIANS 14:33 NCV

God of peace, meet me here. Fill my mind with the clarity of your wisdom. Flood my heart with the peace of your presence. Keep me close to your love and do not let me go. Where I am rushing around in anxious fear, breathe calm into my being. I want to move in the spacious rest of your perspective with peace as my current.

I breathe in the awareness of your nearness now, closing my eyes and tuning in to all that is present in this moment. There is enough peace, enough joy, enough love, enough patience, enough kindness, and enough grace. I turn my attention to you over and over again until my heart is at perfect rest in your faithfulness.

I trade my worries for the Lord's peace. I give him my anxiety and receive his confident rest. I trust that all the Lord is and does is all I need. I have everything I require here and now. This is true in the next moment and all following moments.

The Door

"I am the way, the truth, and the life.
No one can come to the Father except through me."

JOHN 14:6 NLT

Christ Jesus, I come to you today with no hesitation. I bring with me everything that once kept me at an arm's length. I want to be as open with you as you are with me. I hide nothing and hold nothing back, and I know that you will meet me with the fullness of your mercy.

I remember how you said that the Father is merciful as shown through the parable of the prodigal son. I come through you, Jesus, to the open arms of my heavenly Father. I follow you, for you are the way, the truth, and the life. You are my vision, my guiding light, and my open door. Here I am, Lord!

There is no other hope stronger than the hope of Christ living in me. He is the doorway to the Father, to the endless love of his kingdom, and to the home I have longed for. I press in to know him more today.

Filled with Kindness

The Lord is righteous in everything he does;
he is filled with kindness.
The Lord is near to all who call on him,
yes, to all who call on him in truth.

PSALM 145:17-18 NLT

Righteous Lord, I am astounded by your kindness over and
over again. Thank you for being near to all who call out to
you. I have called on you before, and I won't stop. You are
my holy hope, my closest confidant, and the one whom I
trust more than any other.

When there is no one else to turn to, you are near. When
my friends and family are unavailable, you never leave me.
You are closer than all others, and I will not stop feasting
on the kindness of your merciful heart toward me. Make me
even more aware of your presence today as I lean on you.
You are my everything.

*The Lord is full of kindness and righteous in everything he
does. He will never abandon me in my time of need, and he
won't ever leave me in times of peace. He is the one I call
on in both my trouble and my triumph. I rely on him.*

Overflowing Compassion

The LORD is gracious and compassionate,
slow to anger and rich in love.
The LORD is good to all;
he has compassion on all he has made.

PSALM 145:8-9 NIV

Compassionate One, you are better than the most honorable men and women who walk this earth. Your character is flawless, and your wisdom is unmarred by bitterness or apathy. You are full of loyal love and endlessly patient with us; you never deplete your resources of compassion. What a wonder it is that you are so patient with us! You do not deal with us as we deserve. You give us your mercy.

Thank you for these glimpses into your nature as you draw us to your heart with kindness. Even your correction is laced with love. May I become more and more like you as I fellowship with you in spirit and truth.

The Lord is good to all. He does not pick and choose whom he will show mercy toward. He is endlessly compassionate. I get to fill up on his love, and I can be compassionate and merciful from the overflow of his love alive in me.

Restorer

You open the eyes of the blind
and you fully restore those bent over with shame.
You love those who love and honor you.

PSALM 146:8 TPT

Redeemer, you lift the burden of disgrace from those who look to you. Lift mine today. Please light up any shadows of shame with the radiance of your love. I want to walk in the freedom of your mercy. Who you say I am is more important than what anyone else thinks of me. There is no condemnation in your presence, and there is no hopelessness in your heart toward me. What a liberating truth!

I give you all the baggage that I have carried around for far too long. Lift my countenance with your words of life and truth. Speak to me, Lord, and I will come alive in you.

I love and honor the Lord, and I will not keep beating myself up for something that he does not hold against me. I give him all my shame and the defeating thoughts that spin around my mind. He will fully restore me in his love as I yield it all to him.

Delighted

The Lord delights in those who fear him,
who put their hope in his unfailing love.

PSALM 147:11 NIV

Victorious Lord, I trust you with everything in my life.
Battles seem to arise from out of nowhere, but nothing
surprises you. You hear the rumblings of every plot, and
you make provisions with your great mercy.

I put my hope in your unfailing love, and I won't stop. You
are the one who leads me through dark nights of the soul
and who keeps me safe in storms where winds blow and
waves swell. You are the one who created me, and you
will keep me in your perfect peace even when I can't see a
way out. Today I hold on to you, my living hope. Keep me
secure in your merciful love.

*The Lord delights in my trust. He delights in my hope. He
delights in who I am. He delights in me. How could I but
delight in him? He is my true joy, my overwhelming peace,
and my firmest hope. I will delight in him.*

Generous Giving

Give generously to them and do so without a grudging heart; then because of this the Lord your God will bless you in all your work and in everything you put your hand to.

DEUTERONOMY 15:10 NIV

King of kings, you are generous in all you do. I want to reflect your bigheartedness in the way I live my life. Where I am stingy, give me a broader perspective of your abundance. Where I hoard resources to myself, fill me with your compassion to give what I can.

I offer you authority over my time, my emotional capacity, and my belongings so I may follow your instructions to share my gifts in meaningful ways. I know that you are liberal in your love, and I want to reflect you in my relationships and my actions. I will practice giving from a cheerful heart, looking for ways to bless others. I want to stretch this muscle and become more and more like you.

The Lord is generous with me, so I will be generous with others. I will not be quick to self-protect when I see a need I can meet. I will be open-hearted and freely offer what I can. I know that God will honor it.

Chosen

"You didn't choose me. I chose you. I appointed you to go and produce lasting fruit, so that the Father will give you whatever you ask for, using my name."

JOHN 15:16 NLT

Lord, how could I begin to thank you for choosing me? You lift the pressure from my shoulders while reminding me that you chose me before I even knew about you. Thank you for your merciful kindness which reaches out to me my whole life long.

I can't stay away from you. I will build my life upon the foundation of your love, and I give you permission to do what needs to be done to refine my heart in your mercy. I want you more than I want my comfort. I want to know you more than I want to stay the same. Fill my life with your spiritual fruit and wake my sleeping heart with your living love.

I have been chosen by God himself to be his own. I am his heir, and I come with the confidence of a beloved child to my loving Father today. I won't hold anything from him, for he hasn't withheld anything from me.

My Defense

The LORD is my strength and my defense;
he has become my salvation.
He is my God, and I will praise him,
my father's God, and I will exalt him.

EXODUS 15:2 NIV

Defender, I praise you! I am fearfully and wonderfully made. I am carefully kept in the refuge of your loving kindness. You are my salvation, and you are my hope in every season of the soul.

I know that you will continue to come through for me. As long as I breathe, you are not finished with me. You are still sowing seeds of mercy into the soil of my life. You are still working all things together for my good and for your glory. I trust you, Lord.

The Lord is my defense. He is my strength. Jesus is my salvation. He is my God, and I will not hold back my praise from him today. I lavish my worship on him, and I trust him wholeheartedly with every part of my life.

Listen to My Prayer

The LORD does not listen to the wicked,
but he hears the prayers of those who do right.

PROVERBS 15:29 NCV

Lord, listen to my prayer as I offer it to you today. My heart longs for a fresh touch of your mercy right now. You see the end and the beginning, and you know every intention before it is a conscious thought in my mind. You are so merciful, and I know that you will answer my cries when I call out to you.

Lord, I will not let shame or guilt keep me from offering you my whole heart. Even when I royally mess up, you receive me when I return to you. I am yours today, Lord, and I openly lay out my concerns, disappointments, and hopes before you. Please answer me as I look to you.

The Lord hears the prayers of those who call out to him. He recognizes my humble heart, and he responds to my prayers. I won't hold back anything from him today.

Sewn to the Vine

"I am the vine; you are the branches.
If you remain in me and I in you,
you will bear much fruit;
apart from me you can do nothing."

JOHN 15:5 NIV

Source, I would wither if not connected to you. Though I may try to build a life on my own, fruit only grows when I am connected to you. I don't need to strive to see your work through my life when I'm sewn into your vine. Keep me from trying to go my own way and remind me of the goodness of relying on you. I know that you are the source of every good thing.

I want my life to be a garden of your kingdom fruit. Prune me, support me, and do what you will to keep me producing your fruit in my life.

There is no greater source than the Lord. I will remain in him, and he remains in me. The good fruits of love, joy, peace, patience, kindness, goodness, faithfulness, and self-control reflect his life alive in me. I won't stop leaning on him.

Transformation Is Coming

Behold, I tell you a mystery:
We shall not all sleep, but we shall all be changed.

1 CORINTHIANS 15:51 NKJV

Redeemer, thank you for the promise of coming transformation. I'm so grateful for the ways in which you refresh and restore me in during tension of waiting. I know the day is coming when every tear will be wiped away and every traumatic experience will be a memory.

You are so much better than the current state of this world testifies. Your mercy is unending, and I know that your power will come in fullness when you, Christ, finally return. I can't wait until I am living in the fullness of your kingdom come. Encourage my heart in hope as you minister to me through the grace of your presence today.

Even though I can't escape the trials of this world, I know that there is a promise of coming redemption and restoration for all things. I put my hope in Christ and in that day even while living in the reality of his presence with me now.

Heavenly Hope

It will happen in a moment, in the blink of an eye, when the last trumpet is blown. For when the trumpet sounds, those who have died will be raised to live forever. And we who are living will also be transformed.

1 Corinthians 15:52 NLT

Heavenly Father, though grief is a necessary valley to walk through in this life, I know that will not always be the case. My heavenly hope is the eternal transformation that will come when your kingdom reigns in fullness. I have already been welcomed into your kingdom, and I catch glorious glimpses of your wonderful love, power, and joy through your Spirit.

Give me tenacity, compassion, grit, and grace to follow you all the days of my life. I know that as I choose to yield to your path of love, it will be worth it.

Everything will change in a moment when Christ returns for his bride. I want to be found in him, living a life of love in every moment, every day, and every season of my life. I declare that I belong to the Lord, and he is mine.

Victory in Christ

Thanks be to God!
He gives us the victory through our Lord Jesus Christ.
Stand firm. Let nothing move you.
Always give yourselves fully to the work of the Lord,
because you know that your labor in the Lord
is not in vain.

1 CORINTHIANS 15:57-58 NIV

Lord Jesus, I want to stand firm in your victory. You demonstrated the power of your resurrection and life when you rose from the grave three days after your crucifixion. You defeated the grave; the power of death is helpless against your love.

I will stand firm here, rooted in the merciful kindness of your heart. You are the one I have built my life upon, and I remain firm on the solid rock of your nature. I refocus my vision on you, Jesus, the perfecter of my faith. I align my heart with yours, and I depend on your empowering grace to help me through your Spirit.

I declare that Christ's victory is my own. There is no sin, no shame cycle, no trauma, and no curse that can stand against the power of his resurrection life in me. I am free indeed, and I will live my life unabashedly for his love.

Filled with Joy

You make known to me the path of life;
you will fill me with joy in your presence,
with eternal pleasures at your right hand.

PSALM 16:11 NIV

Good Father, in the delight of your heart, I find my home. Every time your Spirit moves within me, I feel the peace, joy, and acceptance of your great love. There is no substitute for the grace and mercy I have found in you. There is no end to your pleasure, and there is no lack of kindness in your countenance.

I come to you freely today, heart laid bare and arms wide open to receive the riches of your presence. Fill me with the treasures that you freely bestow on your children. Give me your hopeful perspective over the unknowns that have my heart twisting in fear. Your ways are so much better than my own, and I trust you to take care of me.

The Lord is good to all who call on him. I will find greater pleasure and delight in his love than anywhere else in this world. He is the source of every good thing in my life, and I will give him praise!

Joy Will Come Again

"Now is your time of grief, but I will see you again and you will rejoice, and no one will take away your joy."

JOHN 16:22 NIV

Comforter, through the dark nights of great loss where grief overtakes every other emotion, it is difficult to remember what the light of day feels like. Still, I trust that as I wade through the depths of grief, I will see the dawn of another day. The sun will shine again, and joy, relief, and hope will be mine. Even though I walk through the valley of the shadow of death, I won't fear a thing, for you are with me.

Just as the psalmist prayed, so do I. I trust you to walk with me, to guide me, and to comfort me. I trust you.

Joy is not a futile thing to be lost in seasons of sadness. Joy is greater than fleeting happiness. As my capacity for sorrow broadens, so does my capacity for joy, hope, and love. I will open my heart to the Spirit's unceasing joy.

Majestic Strength

Splendor and majesty are before him;
strength and joy are in his dwelling place.

1 CHRONICLES 16:27 NIV

Majestic One, if strength and joy are in your dwelling place, that is where I want to be today. Fill me with your powerful presence and draw me near to your heart with your gracious compassion. I need you more than I can express.

When my heart is filled with sorrow, anxiety, or hesitation, I know that you are still full of joy, confidence, and love. Fill me up with the power of your mercy and transform me with your pure perspective. Give me your strength in place of my weakness, Lord. I'm leaning on you instead of relying on my own waning resources. I'm very aware of my need, Lord! Meet me with the fullness of your presence as I look to you; flood me with your life-giving love yet again.

I declare that no matter what I woke up feeling today, no matter how my day has gone, there is fullness of joy and strength in the Lord's presence. I have access to this abundance here and now.

Submit Your Plans

Commit your actions to the L<small>ORD</small>,
and your plans will succeed.

P<small>ROVERBS</small> 16:3 <small>NLT</small>

Lord, as I make my plans, I won't forget to include you. I know that I can make my plans, but things rarely go the way I expect. I trust that you know better and that you are not upset by changing details. I trust that you will continue to work all things out for my good. I trust that you always have solutions to the challenges I can't foresee. I know that you are wise; you will not leave me on my own.

As I plan for my future, I will not hold too tightly to my fantasies or ideals. I will let my goals propel me, but I will also let the unforeseen challenges press me further into you as I persevere. Lead me in your truth and guide me with your mercy. I submit it all to you, knowing you are good and will never change from being good.

My heart trusts that the Lord will guide me through every battle and every triumph. He will never leave me on my own. Even as I make my plans, I let my greatest expectation be God's goodness.

Great Confidence

"Everything I've taught you is so that the peace which is in me will be in you and will give you great confidence as you rest in me. For in this unbelieving world you will experience trouble and sorrows, but you must be courageous, for I have conquered the world!"

JOHN 16:33 TPT

Prince of Peace, I come to you looking for rest for my soul, mind, and body. As I rest, fill me with the strength I need to courageously move through trials and troubles that arise. Your grace is more than enough for each of my relationships, my responsibilities, and my hopes. You are more than enough for me.

In every season of the soul, you are my great confidence. There is no one else I trust more than you. I look to your Word for encouragement, and I press into your presence for hope today. Do not disappoint, Lord. I turn toward you, and I wait for your Spirit's help.

The Lord is my great confidence, and it will not be shaken; he is unchanging. I trust him with all that comes, and I trust him to protect me. I can do hard things with grit and grace, for he is my courage.

Give Thanks

Give thanks to the LORD, for he is good
his love endures forever.

1 CHRONICLES 16:34 NIV

Loving Lord, I give thanks for this new day. For breath in my lungs, I give you thanks. For the sun's rays and rain's refreshment, I give thanks. For all that is, I give thanks. For every detail that I normally overlook in my haste, I give thanks. For the ability to work, to relate, and to love another day, I am so very grateful. For all that was and will be, thank you!

As I give you my time and attention today, may I not take anything for granted. You are good, your love endures forever, and you are full of restoration and redemption power. I search for your hidden mercies in my life like a child searches the ground for treasures. I know that I will find what I'm looking for.

I declare that there are a multitude of reasons to give thanks today. I freely acknowledge and pour out my gratitude to the Lord, and I will not wait for another moment to do it. As I cultivate gratitude, it will grow.

Heart Searcher

The LORD does not see as man sees;
for man looks at the outward appearance,
but the LORD looks at the heart.

1 SAMUEL 16:7 NKJV

Sovereign God, you see past our facades into the truth of our hearts. I rest in the confidence that you really know me. You know my heart, and you honor it. You heal my wounds and my brokenness; you make me whole in your incomparable love.

Look close today, Lord, and reveal what you see within me. Speak your truth over my life. Let me in on your perspective. I know that with you are the words of life. I want to unfold and awaken to you like a flower turns its petals toward the sun. Shine on me, and let the shadows flee from my heart in your glorious presence.

The Lord does not need me to dress up or pretend to be anything other than what I am. He sees my heart, knows my intentions, and breathes hope into my dreams. My confidence is in knowing him and knowing I am fully known and loved. I will seek to be more like him today, looking past outward appearances to see a person's true worth.

May

I pray that your hearts will be flooded with light so that you can understand the confident hope he has given to those he called—his holy people who are his rich and glorious inheritance.

EPHESIANS 1:18 NLT

Always Available

Because you are close to me and always available,
my confidence will never be shaken,
for I experience your wrap-around presence
every moment.

PSALM 16:8 TPT

Spirit of God, I believe that you are, as the psalmist said, "close to me and always available." Even now, as I read these words, you are as close to me as you ever have been. You are as available to me as you were or ever will be. You are ready to answer me. Ready to help me. Ready to heal me. Ready to comfort me.

Spirit, breathe your life into me now. Give me what I long for here in your presence. Your all-encompassing presence is my courage. Enlighten my perspective and reveal how close you are right now. I need you. I want more of you. I love you.

My confidence is not in how capable I am. My true confidence is in the Spirit of God who is always with me, always available, and so very near. I will go through my day with the awareness of his nearness.

Surrendered Hearts

"The eyes of the LORD move to and fro throughout the earth that He may strongly support those whose heart is completely His. You have acted foolishly in this. Indeed, from now on you will surely have wars."

2 CHRONICLES 16:9 NASB

Lord, may my heart remain wholly submitted to you. You are better than anything I could achieve alone in this life. I have known heartache and I have known blessing; you are greater, bigger, and better than any and all of it. Your power knows no bounds, and your love can't be broken.

I look to you today for help and hope. I yield to you and your kingdom ways. Come and encourage me from within. Hold me up in the areas I can't support myself. I will not give myself over to the foolishness of pride. I humble myself before you. You are my only sure and lasting hope.

My heart yields to the King of kings and Lord of lords. His ways are the ways I follow. I clothe myself in humility and trust the Lord to support me, lead me, and never let me go.

Search Me

"I the Lord search the heart and examine the mind,
to reward each person according to their conduct,
according to what their deeds deserve."

JEREMIAH 17:10 NIV

Yahweh, search my heart and examine my mind. I know
that you know me through and through. You parse the
good from the bad. You have clothed me in the mercy of
your Son, and my redemption is in the power of his blood.
I don't stand on my own merit but on who you say that
I am. Your love is purer and your vision clearer than my
own. Where I find a plethora of faults within my heart,
you are uprooting the lies and replacing them with your
truth. When you say that I am loved, you do not put any
conditions upon it.

I am yours, Lord, and I will not let fear keep me from being
completely open with you. I long for a fresh touch of your
mercy on my mind, transforming my thoughts in your
peace. I long for a revelation of your exceeding goodness
to refresh my heart in your incomparable nature. Do what
you will with me today.

The Lord sees me, knows me, and loves me completely.
Hallelujah!

Mountain-moving Faith

"If you have faith like a grain of mustard seed, you will say to this mountain, 'move from here to there,' and it will move, and nothing will be impossible for you."

MATTHEW 17:20 ESV

Powerful One, how I long to move in the power of your presence through faith. Increase my faith as you continue to follow through in faithfulness in my life and in the world around me. Give me eyes to see where you are working, ears to hear what you are saying, and boldness to move as you call me to.

I don't want to shrink back at the mountains looming in my path. I want to walk with confidence knowing that as I do, your faith alive in me will move obstacles. Do what only you can do; transform me with the power of your love to walk in bold faith.

My faith is not in myself but in God, the Creator of the universe. The same God who said "let there be light" will honor the prayers I pray in faith.

Come Together

"If two or three people come together in my name,
I am there with them."

MATTHEW 18:20 NIV

Present One, thank you for the promise of your presence
as we gather together in your name. I know that you will
never leave or forsake me. I also know that you never fail to
show up in power, mercy, and grace when we gather even
in the smallest groups.

I wasn't created to do life alone, and I wasn't meant to
struggle through grief on my own either. I was meant to
share my joys in relationship with others. I was created to
celebrate with those who are reveling in your goodness
in their lives. Give me a heart that seeks connection over
isolation and understanding over offense. I want to know
you in all my relationships.

*Jesus promises to be with those who gather in his name.
His love makes a way for us to be strengthened and
encouraged in fellowship. I will connect with others in his
name today and watch to see how he moves.*

Perfect and Trustworthy

As for God, His way is perfect;
the word of the LORD is proven;
He is a shield to all who trust in Him.

PSALM 18:30 NKJV

God, there is none more trustworthy than you. Your Word is your vow, and you will never break it. What you have promised in loyal love can never be revoked. I get discouraged by the broken trust of my relationships, and I know that is not how you work. You do not deceive, and you do not hide your intentions. You are perfect in all of your ways. I don't look for perfection in those around me; in your flawlessness, I find true confidence.

When others fail me, may I see clearly that your faithfulness never wavers. May I have abundant mercy to extend because of the amount of mercy you freely offer me. Thank you for being a shield in this life. I hide in your unfailing love.

God will never fail. His ways are my perfect provision. He will never let me down, and he will never let me go. He is perfect in all his ways and worthy of my trust.

Armed with Strength

God arms me with strength,
and he makes my way perfect.
He makes me as surefooted as a deer,
enabling me to stand on mountain heights.
He trains my hands for battle;
he strengthens my arm to draw a bronze bow.

PSALM 18:32-34 NLT

Perfect Lord, you are the one I cling to in my time of need. You are the one I look to in times of uncertainty. You are the one! Give me strength when I am quaking in indecision and fear. Give me clarity for my confusion. Give me peace for my anxiety. Please give me yourself. Train me for what lies ahead as I trustingly follow you. Teach me with your wisdom and build me up in your truth.

I'm so grateful I never have to go it alone. Even though I fail myself and others, I know that you will never fail. You teach me the strength of tenacity and the value of mercy as you meet with me.

There is no need to fear when I have God by my side. He will not abandon me in my hour of need. He will make a way through, and he will give me the strength I need as I rely on him. Yes, he will do it!

Sought After

"The Son of Man came to seek and to save the lost."

LUKE 19:10 NIV

Lord, I'm so grateful that there is nothing lost that can't be found by you. There is nothing hidden from you. You see everything clearly. You know everyone as well as you know yourself. Why would I put conditions on others and their healing when you don't?

Teach me to be more like you as you transform me in your living love. Your mercy is full of power to restore and to redeem even the most far-gone situation. Nothing is impossible for you, and I believe that you will continue to call believers home to you and gather them with your love. You are fierce and tender. You are merciful and just. You will never give up on the defenseless, and you won't leave the vulnerable. Thank you, Jesus.

What was lost is found in Jesus. Nothing is outside of the realm of his loving kindness. His power can make the broken whole, the disheartened encouraged, and the grief-stricken hopeful.

Give to the Lord

Whoever is generous to the poor lends to the Lᴏʀᴅ,
and he will repay him for his deed.

PROVERBS 19:17 ESV

Generous Father, may my heart reflect your generosity, and
may my life reflect your humility and mercy. Everything I
have originated in you, and it is my joy to partner with your
love and give to those in need without expecting anything
in return. I know that you will reward me; you are my
reward. I do not look for recompense from those who are
just trying to get by.

I will stretch the boundaries of my faith by opening my
heart in more love, looking for ways to strengthen the
vulnerable and to encourage the heartbroken. I will not
be apathetic or self-serving. Your love always reaches
outward, and I will do the same.

*The Lord gives freely to all he has made. I will also be
generous with my own resources, looking for ways to serve
and bless those in need. I will give my money but also my
time. I will look for ways to be a blessing today.*

Abandoned Love

When you live a life of abandoned love,
surrendered before the awe of God,
here's what you'll experience:
Abundant life. Continual protection.
And complete satisfaction!

PROVERBS 19:23 TPT

Holy One, I want my life to be like this proverb. I want to live a life of abandoned love before you. I don't love you simply because it's what I know I should do. I love you because you loved me first. You love me still. You love me relentlessly. You never stop filling my life with your mercy. You never leave. You never give up. You never hurt me. You heal me, you build me up, and you encourage me. Even in your correction, I taste the purity of your loving kindness.

There is nothing that you do without love, so why would I attempt to live any differently? Fill me up so that I can live out of the overflow of your mercy, extending it in every circumstance, in every relationship, in abundant measure. Oh, how I love you!

The Lord is my complete satisfaction. I find wholeness where he meets me, abides in me, and fills me. I am whole, and I am wholly alive in him. I will live with abandoned love before his face.

He Lives

> "I know that my Redeemer lives, and he will stand upon
> the earth at last. And after my body has decayed,
> yet in my body I will see God! I will see him for myself."
>
> JOB 19:25-26 NLT

Redeemer, I believe that you are alive. You will stand
upon the earth again. You will come back for all you have
claimed as your own. You are coming back for a ready
bride You are coming to restore, reclaim, and refurbish the
earth. I want to be found in you all the days of my life with
this living hope ringing in my chest. I know that whether
this day comes in my lifetime or not, I will see you. I will see
you for myself.

Until then, Spirit, be as real to me as the air in my lungs.
Fellowship with me as I look to you. I am lovesick for you,
Lord. I can't wait until we are standing face to face as every
trouble, trial, and heartbreak becomes a memory.

The Lord is coming to rule and to reign. He is coming again.
Even now, he is alive! His life in mine is my sustenance and
my strength, and he gives me hope for tomorrow.

Greater than Humanity

"Humanly speaking, it is impossible.
But with God everything is possible."

MATTHEW 19:26 NLT

God, I know that with you anything is possible. You are powerful in all your ways, and your love makes everything better. Meet me in the midst of my unknowns, my messes, and my questions with the power of your mercy. Weave all my frayed edges together with your thread that won't ever tear.

When I look at areas of impossibility in my life and hear your voice calling me to be brave and trust you, I will yield my heart to you. I will push through the fear and trust that you will follow through on what you say you will do. You are faithful, and I know that you aren't finished working your good out in my life yet.

Nothing is impossible for God. No matter how stumped or discouraged I may feel, God is confident in his love. I will trust him more than I trust human logic.

So Much Mercy

Once you were not a people,
but now you are the people of God;
once you had not received mercy,
but now you have received mercy.

1 PETER 2:10 NIV

Merciful Father, thank you for choosing me as your own. I am your child, and no one can take that away from me. You have called me into your family and covered me with the seal of your Son. There is nothing I need to do to earn my place here. I am yours. I am yours. I am yours. I belong to you!

Thank you for your powerful mercy that makes all things new, including me. You breathe hope into long-forgotten dreams. You give kindness where I was once ashamed. You empower me to love others as your love transforms my very life. You are my source, and I rely on you in all things. You are the firm foundation of my identity, and no one can change or take away what you have done.

I am a child of the King of kings. I am dearly loved, wonderfully accepted, and treated as an heir. There is no shame in my place as child of the living God. He has all I need, and in his kingdom, I have found my true home.

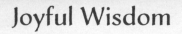

Joyful Wisdom

Wisdom will enter your heart,
and knowledge will fill you with joy.

PROVERBS 2:10 NLT

Lord, I want to be full of your wisdom and knowledge.
You are full of pure peace for those who look to you. You
have solutions for our problems. You have hope for our
disappointments. You have everything we need and so
much more.

I will not waste time on worry. I will not stay stuck in fear.
I come to you, knowing you will instruct me with your
unmatched wisdom. As I do, you give me insight by your
Spirit that I could not attain on my own. Work all things
out, Lord, with the grace of your presence. Fill me with
your knowledge that I may be full of joy today. Your truth is
unrivaled.

*The wisdom of God is better than rubies, gold, or silver. I
will search for his heavenly treasures, and my life will be
enriched with his leadership and insight.*

Spirit Help

What we have received is not the spirit of the world.
We have received the Spirit who is from God. The Spirit
helps us understand what God has freely given us.

1 CORINTHIANS 2:12 NIRV

Holy Spirit, I am so grateful to have you, to know you,
and to be filled with you. I am so grateful for the tangible
peace of your presence. I am thankful for the joy of your
nearness. I can't begin to thank you for all the ways you
enrich my life. I have received you, and I will press into you
to know more of the kingdom of my God and Father.

Reveal the wonderful truths of God's nature. Open my
eyes to see the glimpses of his glory that are all around.
I don't want to wander aimlessly, thinking I know what is
important but actually missing the point. Help me, Spirit; I
yield to you.

*The Spirit of God is full of love, joy, peace, patience, and
kindness. There is hope, there is encouragement, and there
is renewed vision in his presence. I will look to him first,
foremost, and often.*

Still Faithful

If we are not faithful, he will still be faithful,
because he must be true to who he is.

2 TIMOTHY 2:13 NCV

Faithful Father, I love this verse more than I can say. The reminder that your faithfulness is not dependent on my faith is liberating. There is nothing I can do to make you stray from your promises. There is nothing I can say to make you change your mind. Nothing!

I am filled with gratitude for your incomparable mercy. Thank you for following through on every promise you make. I know nothing can make you break your covenant of mercy. You are true to who you are regardless of how I act. May I become more like you: consistent and loving in all I do, faithful to my word and to mercy. I want to reflect you in my humanity even as I give up all ideals of perfection in myself. You are gracious; may I be also.

The Lord is faithful. Even when I am unfaithful, he is faithful. I will not lower my expectations of his goodness, and I will not use any excuse for foolishness. I will live in the liberty of his love with gratitude and praise on my lips.

More Desire

God is working in you, giving you the desire
and the power to do what pleases him.

PHILIPPIANS 2:13 NLT

Great God, thank you for your desire inside of me. Thank you for planting within me the longing to know you, to be like you, and to live with your values as my own. By your Spirit, give me the grace and strength I need to keep pursuing you, to keep promoting love, and to be one who seeks true peace than I do my own way. May I be like you as I look for ways to restore and redeem that which has been lost to conflict. I want to be a bridge-maker and a safe harbor for those seeking respite.

What you have already begun in me, Lord, increase. I am doing the work of seeking you, listening to you, and living a life of humble surrender. Do what you do, Lord; do the rest.

Even the desire I have for God is from God himself. It originates in him, and it is a gift. I can do all things through him, for he is my strength and my great reward.

Eternal Promises

The world and its desires pass away,
but whoever does the will of God lives forever.

1 John 2:17 niv

Everlasting One, though life is fleeting, you are eternal.
Your love has no beginning, and it will never reach an
end. No container can bottle up your mercy. I have seen
how temporal this life is, and I am keenly aware of the
short time we have here. In this one beautiful and brutal
life, I want to live with your law of love as my motivation
and vision. Your love always expands and brings us to
life. I want to expand in my understanding of you, in my
expression of your mercy and in my relationship with you.

Keep my eyes coming back to you whenever they stray.
When the weight of the world gets too heavy, lift my
burden and show me the perspective of your vantage. I
need to know you more, Lord. I am yours.

*Everything the Lord does has eternal consequences. I do
everything with his kingdom in mind. Nothing is too trivial
for him, and I know that he is working all things together
for his glory and for my good and for the good of his
children.*

Foundation of Truth

God's truth stands firm like a foundation stone with this
inscription: "The Lord knows those who are his," and
"All who belong to the Lord must turn away from evil."

2 TIMOTHY 2:19 NLT

Lord, thank you for your truth that stands firm. It is the
foundation that I have built my life upon. I belong to you. I
have turned from every form of shame, sin, and foolishness
that seeks its own gain at the expense of others. I have
submitted to your kingdom ways, to your values, and to
your highest law: the law of your love.

I will treat others with the same mercy you extend to me.
I will offer the benefit of the doubt when others throw
curses and judgments. I will go to the margins, and I will
follow your lead in helping the vulnerable. You are better
than any other, and I want to be like you. May your mercy
be clearly expressed through my life.

*The Lord knows who are his, and I am his. No one can fool
him, and no one can convince him of lies. He knows my
heart. I will live fully submitted to his love above all else.*

Christ in Me

My old self has been crucified with Christ. It is no longer I who live, but Christ lives in me. So I live in this earthly body by trusting in the Son of God, who loved me and gave himself for me.

GALATIANS 2:20 NLT

Christ, you are the life within me. You are inner power that lets me choose to persevere when I would rather escape. You never ran from pain, and I won't either. I know that the only way to truly get through any situation is to go through it.

I will stop trying to run away from the trials and troubles that keep coming up. Instead, I will lean on you and trust your wisdom, strength, and mercy to empower and help me through. I trust you more than I trust myself. I trust you more than I trust any other.

I am not ruled by coping mechanisms or cycles of trauma any longer. It is by Christ's love that I have been set free, and it is his life within mine that empowers me to live according to his ways and purposes. I am an overcomer because Christ has already overcome.

Offerings of Wisdom

He gives wisdom to the wise and knowledge
to the discerning.

DANIEL 2:21 NIV

Sovereign Lord, you know how much I want to know
you. I want to live according to your wisdom and ways. I
have spent time learning your voice, your tone, and your
message. I know that your nature is pure, constant, and
overwhelmingly beautiful. I will never find another like you.

Even as I grow in wisdom, continue to reveal more of
yourself to me. I long to walk in the light of your freedom
all the days of my life. Give me more discernment as I look
to you for guidance. I don't look for shortcuts or quick
getaways. I know that you lead me to life, to abundant life,
and I choose to follow you.

*There is nothing that stumps the Lord. There are no
problems too big for him. I declare that his wisdom is
accessible to me today through fellowship with his Spirit.
His knowledge is available to me as I seek him.*

Honored

"Those who honor me I will honor."

1 Samuel 2:30 niv

Lord, I choose to honor you with my life. Even in my mistakes and misgivings, I keep turning to you. I don't want to live with pride as my protection. There is no need to protect myself against you. I humbly submit my heart to yours knowing your wisdom is sweeter, purer, and truer than any other.

I am open to your leading. I am submitted to your teaching. I honor you with my life, for you are worthy of it. You are my Creator, my friend, and my confidant. You never leave me, and I won't abandon you either. May today be full of moments of free fellowship between my spirit and yours. I honor you, Lord, for you are the most important thing to me.

Today I will not hold back from the Lord. As I honor him with my trust, my longings, and my life, he will honor me with his fellowship and faithfulness. He is so very good, and he is worthy of all I could ever offer him.

Hidden Treasure

If you call out for insight
and raise your voice for understanding,
if you seek it like silver
and search for it as for hidden treasures,
then you will understand the fear of the Lord
and find the knowledge of God.

PROVERBS 2:3-5 ESV

Yahweh, I call out for insight today. I raise my voice to you for understanding. I'm seeking your perspective more than my own gain today. I am looking for your discernment like I would for hidden treasure. I know that your wisdom is written into creation; it's all around me in the order of the world. It's in the cycles of the seasons. It's in the mysteries of the universe and in the beauty of nature.

I am astounded by your creativity, and I am drawn to know you more through the revelations I have already received. I want to understand you more today. Please reveal yourself to me in new and invigorating ways. Show me what I have not yet understood and blow my mind with your goodness.

The Lord is better than we could ever imagine. He is more creative, more intentional, and more merciful than we can comprehend. I will search for imprints of his kindness in the world around me, and I know I will find his wisdom as I pursue it.

Living Stones

You are living stones that God is building into his spiritual temple. What's more, you are his holy priests. Through the mediation of Jesus Christ, you offer spiritual sacrifices that please God.

1 Peter 2:5 nlt

Holy One, thank you for offering me access to you through your Son. I come boldly before your throne, even more boldly than the priests of the holy place, for Jesus has torn the curtain that separated your presence from the people. There is no separation between you and I any longer. Thank you!

I come to you through Jesus Christ, and I submit my life as a spiritual sacrifice. I honor you even as you set me in a place of honor in your kingdom. I give you access to all my life and hold nothing back from you. I worship you with every part of me. You have my time, attention, resources, and the sacrifice of my praise. Even in pain, I know that you are with me. You are the Redeemer, and you are not finished. Thank you for using my little life to display your mercy. Thank you for your love that doesn't see it as a sacrifice. I am undone before you.

Through Christ, I have been met by love. I have been washed by mercy. I am a part of God's kingdom, a living stone of his temple. He will use my life to increase his kingdom on this earth.

Oaks of Righteousness

Let your roots grow down into him,
and let your lives be built on him.
Then your faith will grow strong
in the truth you were taught,
and you will overflow with thankfulness.

Colossians 2:7 nlt

Rock of Ages, you are the foundation of my life. Your love is the soil that the roots of my heart grow in. Here, in fellowship with your presence, I am cultivated by your mercy. I grow stronger in the grace of your Spirit. I come alive in your delight. You are my sustenance and strength. You are my hope and my deliverer. No one can pluck me from your orchard.

Continue to prune me as needed. I humble myself in your care. I know that as I remain rooted and established in you, my life will grow your Spirit's fruit. There is an abundance of gratitude within me, and I must pour it out on you today.

I am rooted in the kingdom of my Father. There, I come alive. My life is built upon his love, and I will not be moved. My faith will grow strong in his truth, and gratitude will overflow from my heart and life.

Keep Doing Good

He will give eternal life to those who keep on doing good, seeking after the glory and honor and immortality that God offers.

ROMANS 2:7 NLT

God, I won't give up doing the good I know to do. Jesus was so very clear about the values we should live by. I'm so grateful Jesus wasn't prescriptive with his advice. He spoke in parables so that we would rely on relationship to know the truth.

The values of the kingdom are clear. I want to live my life built on your love. I want to be a promoter of peace and of love. I want to call others in instead of excluding anyone. I want to be a proponent of unity, not disengagement. I will do the good I know to do, and I will keep pressing into knowing you more through your Spirit. There is no lack in your presence, and I trust that I will find everything I'm looking for there.

I declare that there is good for me to do here and now. I don't need to wonder about what impact my life will one day make; I make an impact in each interaction and in every movement toward love and humility in my relationships. I will follow through on what I said I would do and reflect you in my consistency.

From the Dust

"He raises the poor from the dust and lifts the needy from the ash heap; he seats them with princes and has them inherit a throne of honor. For the foundations of the earth are the Lord's; on them he has set the world."

1 Samuel 2:8 niv

Restorer, thank you for raising the needy from the ashes and the poor from the dust. Your character gives me so much hope. Even where I have known disappointment, I know there is an opportunity for your goodness to meet me with redemption.

You are so good at weaving things together to make a beautiful masterpiece. Do it with my life, Lord, even with the pieces that seem extraneous and worthless to me. I know that nothing goes wasted in your hands. Raise me from the ashes, and I will raise others with me as I am brought up. I am devoted to you.

I need not fear what today will bring, for God is with me. He will not let me be overtaken by anything or anyone. He is my peace, and he is the builder of my future. I will live with his generosity as my own, and I will partner with him in lifting the needy from the rubble of their lives.

Gift of Grace

It is by grace you have been saved, through faith—
and this is not from yourselves, it is the gift of God—
not by works, so that no one can boast.

EPHESIANS 2:8-9 NIV

Gracious God, thank you for the gift of your grace that has delivered me from my shame. You have taken every fear of failure and said that you do not expect perfection from me but rather simple submission. I receive the gift of your mercy, and I let my faith grow by the river of your love. Be my source and my supply.

When I am disheartened and discouraged in myself and others, remind me that you are better to us than we are to ourselves. Your plans are better, your vision clearer, and you have goodness in store. I can't earn my way in or out of your love, and I am so grateful.

I can never earn or lose the grace of God. It is a free gift that I receive from him. I take it, and I get to partner with him in extending it to others. What a gift. What a joy!

Glorious Preparations

What no eye has seen, nor ear heard,
nor the heart of man imagined,
what God has prepared for those who love him.

1 CORINTHIANS 2:9 ESV

Great One, it is a relief to me that no one can imagine the extent of your workmanship. What you have prepared for those who love you is infinitely better than anyone could dream. Children dream and imagine freely, but as we grow, we are taught to stick to what is real and plausible as we accept the limits of logic.

Though we can't escape responsibilities in the world, I never want to lose my sense of wonder and creativity. When I step into cathedrals and forests, when I look across the ocean or travel down a river, my sense of assurance and awe simultaneously expand. I am able to dream of bigger, better realities. When I look at the starry heavens, my heart awakens with increased possibilities. May I dream bigger even as I realize that my imaginings don't touch the wonders of your reality.

The Lord has prepared things too wonderful for our understanding in his kingdom. He is better, more glorious, and more full of possibilities we could never dream. I will stretch my imagination in him today.

Marvelous Light

You are a chosen race, a royal priesthood, a holy nation,
a people for his own possession, that you may proclaim
the excellencies of him who called you out of darkness
into his marvelous light.

1 Peter 2:9 esv

King of kings, I belong to you. You have called me out
of the shadows and into your marvelous light. Here,
standing in the light of your presence, I come alive. You are
wonderful, and I will tell those around me how wonderful
you are. As I think over my life with you and our journey
together, remind me of the deposits of your kindness I
have forgotten about. Refresh my hope in the faithfulness
of your character. Remind me where you have already
come through in loyal love, where you have never let go,
and where you never gave up even when I had.

You are so much better than I can describe. Let my love
response rise now from the depths of my heart and fill
yours. I love you so!

*I am chosen by God. I am his. I belong to him. I will not
forget what he has done for me. I will share it with others
today, and I will let their encouragement be my own. I will
feast in the light of his faithfulness all the days of my life.*

People of God

You are a chosen people, a royal priesthood, a holy
nation, God's special possession, that you may declare
the praises of him who called you out of darkness
into his wonderful light. Once you were not a people,
but now you are the people of God; once you had not
received mercy, but now you have received mercy.

1 PETER 2:9-10 NIV

God, thank you for calling me your own. Thank you for
freely pouring your mercy out on all in the same abundant
measure. There are no divisions in your kingdom. There is
no division in your love. There is only one kingdom of love.
One kingdom of the Father. One kingdom of the Son. One
kingdom of the Spirit. One kingdom for every tribe, nation,
and language. All together one kingdom.

Thank you for making me a part of this inclusive kingdom
of yours. What a joy and an honor! I will declare your
praises today, not holding back a single thought. You are
worthy of my trust, my praise, and my very life.

*I am a small part of a larger whole. I am filled with the
merciful kindness of the King of kings, and I belong to his
kingdom. I celebrate and will continue to celebrate his
lavish love throughout my day.*

June

"Whatever you ask in prayer,
believe that you have
received it, and it
will be yours."

MARK 11:24 ESV

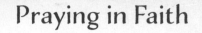

Praying in Faith

"Whatever you ask in prayer, you will receive,
if you have faith."

MATTHEW 21:22 ESV

Precious Savior, your words invite me to request anything in prayer. The promise that I will be given what I ask for is sometimes difficult for me. I do feel blessed that I can simply ask and you will supply, yet I must confess there is a flicker of doubt in my heart. Maybe it is because the key component of prayer is faith. I admit my faith is sometimes timid and therefore not fully put into action.

I want to believe without wavering. Please help me have absolute, irrefutable belief in all you say and in what you can accomplish. I want to end my prayers knowing I will receive all I need from you.

God has given me everything I need: Christ Jesus and faith. He hears my prayers and is sure to answer them. I will come before his throne with complete confidence. I will not doubt. I will seek to please my God by living with certainty that his answer will come. His answers will be given in his wisdom and for my benefit. I will rejoice in the God who answers prayer.

Living Free

> "Remain passionate and free from anxiety and the worries of this life. Then you will not be caught off guard by what happens."
>
> LUKE 21:34 TPT

Father, as I read the online news, my heart is heavy with concern. Our world is in such turmoil, and every day it seems there is a new threat facing us. When I go to bed at night, I wonder what the morning will bring, and it causes sleepless nights.

I know this is not what you want for me, nor is it what I want for myself. If I truly know you hold the future and control the outcome, why am I so disturbed? Help me not to look at circumstances but at you, the only one who has ultimate authority over our present and our eternity.

I know the all-powerful God, and I declare that he is sovereign. Nothing and no one can thwart his plans, for they are set in eternity. I declare that any fear and any weapon forged against me will fall at once. I will live in authority, in confidence, and in absolute peace. I will laugh at the future, for I fully believe in the goodness of the one who holds it.

No More Pain

"He will wipe away every tear from their eyes,
and there will be no more death, sadness, crying,
or pain, because all the old ways are gone."

REVELATION 21:4 NCV

Lord, I pray for everyone I know who is suffering. So many
are sick and experiencing great losses of relationships,
employment, or health. Some have loved ones who have
passed, and my heart aches for them. I also ache over my
own agony, the one you know all too well. I have lived with
this thorn for so long and yet you ask me, in your wisdom,
to continue.

Help me endure. Help me trust you even though I don't
understand. Someday when I am with you, the old will be
no more, and the new will be magnificent. For now, help
me praise you. You love me, and you are transforming me
into the likeness of your Son.

*I declare that there is a day coming. We can't predict its
date, but we can anticipate it with certainty. It is a glorious
day when the absence of pain, sickness, death, and tears
will be abolished for all time. I will live forever without
sorrow, without disability, and without loss. I will flourish for
eternity in the presence of my God and Savior.*

Faithful and True

He who sits on the throne said,
"Behold, I am making all things new."
And He said, "Write, for these words
are faithful and true."

REVELATION 21:5 NASB

Father, when I am on the receiving end of rumors and words that have no truth in them, it feels like a relationship or something inside of me has died. It grieves me that this miscommunication about me was ever conceived, let alone passed along by someone I care for. How could I think that person cared for me?

I long for honesty in other's comments. Please let truth come to light like your words that are always faithful and righteous. Bring reconciliation to our souls. Birth new trust for others in my heart.

My Father's words will never fail. They are trustworthy, sincere, and written for eternity. I believe that a time is coming when he will make all things new. As his forever bride, I will see the triune God in all his glory on the heavenly throne. He saw my forever after with him before time began, but to me it will be a beautiful, bright beginning. Scripture proclaims it, I believe it, and I can't wait for that glorious day!

He Listens

He has not ignored or belittled
the suffering of the needy.
He has not turned his back on them,
but has listened to their cries for help.

PSALM 22:24 NLT

Lord, I confess that I have not always had an attentive ear or a helpful heart for those who are suffering. I get caught up in my daily chores, my job, and my family; I can easily forget that so many are struggling. It is easy to excuse neglect by saying, "I can't save the world," but it is my duty to remember that I can aid someone.

You are my great example, for you never miss a cry for help. You hold the tears of the world in a bottle. Give me eyes to see, ears to hear, and the courage to never turn my back on the needy.

Jesus has given me the power of the Holy Spirit; I can be his hands and feet to all I encounter. I can brighten the day and lighten the load of someone just by noticing and helping. Even a tiny impact can bring some solution to their situation. I am not called to pass by without responding. I am commanded to put others ahead of myself. I will not ignore those who are in need.

God Who Saves

My God is my rock.
I can run to him for safety.
The Lord saves me from those who want to harm me.

2 Samuel 22:3 ncv

Abba, I know I'm not supposed to worry, but sometimes I get scared about my safety in this world. Crazy things happen, and it seems like they are happening more frequently. I find myself questioning whether I want to go to certain events because someone could walk in and end what was brimming with life moments before.

Then I remember who holds me. I know whom I believe in, and I am certain that nothing and no one can thwart what you have planned for me. You are my personal fortress. I am forever safe, every hour of every day, now and forever.

There is nothing to fear. I have no reason to hide, and I will not live anxiously. My life was planned by the Creator before I was even born. I will live boldly so that others will see God in me. I will walk in confidence and joy knowing that my life is held in him. I proclaim that the omnipotent God's watchful eye and strong arms are my security.

Shelter of Forgiveness

This God—his way is perfect;
the word of the Lord proves true;
he is a shield for all those who take refuge in him.

2 SAMUEL 22:31 ESV

God, when I give into temptation, I feel like I've fallen too far once again and despair that I will never change. Held up against your perfection, I want to hide and cover myself in hopes that my wrongdoing will go unnoticed. We both know that is utterly ridiculous, for nothing is hidden from your sight. Your Word reveals my sin and confronts me.

Thankfully, Scripture also teaches me a way out. If I confess, you are faithful to forgive. If I keep your Word in my heart, I can rest assured that its truth will set me on the right path. I acknowledge your ways are perfect, and I want to find solace in your shelter.

I declare the perfection of my Lord's great, all-powerful ways. He alone is good. There is none like him, for he is the one true God. He is my shelter from the storm. He is my deliverer whose arm is mighty to save. I will never be destroyed! I will forever be the victor because I belong to him, and he is faithful.

My Shepherd

The LORD is my shepherd;
I have everything I need.

PSALM 23:1 NCV

Jesus, artists often depict you holding a little lamb sweetly against your cheek. When I look at those pictures, I see you and me. I am your sheep. You are my shepherd: the one who leads me, provides for me, protects me, and lays down his life for me.

When I look at those portraits, everything else fades away. The place where the picture is and the objects that surround it become nothing. You are my everything. All this life has to offer pales in comparison to you. Though all earthly things pass away, you will remain.

I have found all I want, all I need, and all that matters in the Good Shepherd. After realizing that he chose and loved me first, I do not now, nor will I ever, want for anything else but that beautiful truth. I don't deserve Christ, but his grace and love have been freely given to me. I proclaim I belong to him alone, and I am sealed by his Holy Spirit.

Humble Exaltation

"Whoever exalts himself will be humbled,
and whoever humbles himself will be exalted."

MATTHEW 23:12 ESV

Father, I come before you quite ashamed of a certain behavior. I brag a bit. I guess I want to be noticed, to feel like I matter. I want everyone present to really see me. When you answer my prayers and open doors I so desperately want, I quickly forget that it is your doing. I forget that I am simply the vessel. I seek recognition for something I could never bring about with my own strength.

Forgive me for exalting myself and making it appear that your efforts were mine. Please help me give you the praise that is rightfully yours.

I bow humbly before God's mighty throne and declare that without him, I can do nothing. I also proclaim that nothing is impossible with him. In his power, all is accomplished. I praise him for his generosity in allowing me to work in his plans. I know he has plans to prosper me, give me hope, and empower me to work for the good and glory of his kingdom.

Eternal Hope

There is surely a future hope for you,
and your hope will not be cut off.

PROVERBS 23:18 NIV

God, there are days when hope seems to be in short supply. I look at people's faces, and it's like they have given up. They appear devoid of any belief that things will ever get better. So many others are trying to put on a happy face and failing miserably. If only they knew you.

Therein lies my responsibility to share the hope that is mine through Jesus as my Savior. They could surrender to your loving salvation, and they would know there is hope. Help me share your gospel. May those who hear me find their future in Jesus Christ.

I declare with great joy and assurance that there is hope, and that hope is in Jesus! I have a future, secure and sealed, bright and beautiful, that will place me in God's presence for the length of my never-ending days. Nothing can alter that truth, and nothing can steal my hope. All my days are lived with the tremendous guarantee of eternity with my God.

All-Sufficient

God is not a man, that He should lie,
Nor a son of man, that he should repent.
Has he said, and will he not do?
Or has he spoken, and will he not make it good?

NUMBERS 23:19 NKJV

Father, I love our intimacy, but I tend to consider you more often as Abba than Lord God Almighty. I want to worship your majesty but sit on your lap at the same time. I want to remember and acknowledge that you are the all-sufficient God on high. You are the sovereign King, yet you are close enough to count the hairs on my head.

Help me to fully understand your character, to walk in your truth, and rejoice in knowing that all you do is good. Help me praise you as I AM, the Savior of the world and the lover of my soul.

God's ways are higher and greater than mine. In him lie all things pure, faithful, and true. I believe in his good purpose for me and in the inexplicable magnitude of love that he showed by sacrificing his Son for me. Through prayer and the Scriptures, the Holy Spirit will reveal more of God's nature to me and lead me into a deeper relationship with him.

Transforming Renewal

He restores my soul;
He leads me in the paths of righteousness
for His name's sake.

PSALM 23:3 NKJV

When weariness overcomes me, I hear your still, small voice. "Come rest in me. Let me bring refreshment to your soul." Life in you is peace, but existing in this world brings overwhelming challenges. When I have days that bring me down, may they take me to my knees. Help me pour out my heart and receive your restoring assurance that you have conquered all.

Give me the boldness to share with everyone how you, and only you, can bring true salvation. I want others to know the transforming renewal of new life in Christ. Help me live an upright life led by your good plan and for your glory.

There is no rest, no peace, and no salvation outside of my Lord and God. I am fully restored when I sit at his feet and cry out to him in prayer. His path is covered with goodness and uprightness, and he guides me on it with great care and love. For the rest of my days, all I want to do is follow Jesus and bring glory to his holy name.

Protective Guide

Even when I walk through the darkest valley,
I will not be afraid, for you are close beside me.
Your rod and your staff protect and comfort me.

PSALM 23:4 NLT

Father, I confess that some of the dark valleys I've walked through have been of my own choosing. In those times, I'm afraid because I know I have stepped out of your will by succumbing to temptation. Even then, you are right beside me, admonishing me to repent and reminding me that I have nothing to fear.

Your correction is kind yet effective. As I respond to your invitation to turn from sin, I find great comfort in knowing you never have, and never will, leave me for any reason. When I walk through trials that have been allowed by your hand, I know you have already walked ahead. You will guide me, console me, and win the victory on my behalf.

My Father's protective and watchful eye is constantly on me. I declare that there is never anything to fear. I rejoice in his continual presence knowing that nothing and no one can separate us. I receive his correction with gratitude, and I am comforted by the fact that he will always be my wise and holy companion.

Pursued by Love

Why would I fear the future?
For your goodness and love pursue me
all the days of my life.
Then afterward, when my life is through,
I'll return to your glorious presence
to be forever with you!

Psalm 23:6 TPT

Father, sometimes I wish knew more about what tomorrow will bring. Those times are usually surrounded by a situation or complication that is creating fear and stress in my life. When this happens, I want to remember that you hold the future. Because I am yours, you will always be with me in anything that may distress me.

I know all your ways are good. Your love is grand and far beyond my understanding. I want to focus what will certainly happen, not what might happen. What is certain? I have a future forever home in heaven where I will exist with you for eternity.

I declare the Lord God Almighty's goodness and love chase me down daily just to show me how great his affection is for me. I am absolutely elated at the thought of what he has prepared for me once I graduate to heaven. There, I will see his face and worship him always. God has blessed me with his presence on this earth, but I can't wait for the best that is yet to come.

It Is All His

The earth is the Lord's, and everything in it.
The world and all its people belong to him.

PSALM 24:1 NLT

Lord, as I rummage through my things to see what can go to charity, I am dismayed at how much I have accumulated. As I kneel before you, I must confess that I have not been a good steward. I have bought things on a whim that I don't even use. When you have given me all I need, why do I strive for and crave unnecessary things?

On this earth, only people will last eternally. Help me invest in those who have needs instead of piling up the latest hot items for myself. Forgive me for my senseless excess. Help me use what you have generously given me to build your kingdom.

Everything was created by God, for God, and is his alone. I never want to look at anything as belonging solely to me. Instead, I will offer it on his altar to do with as he wishes. I am grateful for the freedom I find when I release everything to the King, the rightful owner of all.

He Is Our Hope

"Keep your hope to the end
and you will experience life and deliverance."

MATTHEW 24:13 TPT

Jesus, it can be a daily struggle to hold on to hope. This world is almost devoid of it. Even though I know my future and the security I have in you, I can get bogged down and deeply affected by the madness in our culture. I am so thankful for your Word that always encourages me, teaches me, and reminds me where my hope comes from.

I know that as I continue to trust in you and the truth of Scripture that you will show me abundant life and eventually rescue me from this fallen world. I am so thankful that I know you, the only true hope.

My hope is in Jesus! There is no other name, and there is no other way; he alone is my salvation. What tremendous peace, what abundant joy to know that he will carry me through this life and one day present me as his own before the Father. I believe in and belong to him, the conqueror of sin and death, the Savior of the world.

Developing Fruit

Use patience and kindness
when you want to persuade leaders
and watch them change their minds
right in front of you.
For your gentle wisdom
will quell the strongest resistance.

PROVERBS 25:15 TPT

Father, thank you for your Word that advises me to be slow to anger, patient, and consider others as more important than myself. I am grateful that your Spirit aids me in those areas. On my own, I would surely fail to exhibit any of those traits. There is wisdom in gentle instruction, kind requests, and respectful presentation. This fruit can win over the hearts of the most skeptical.

I ask for favor and power through your Holy Spirit as I discipline myself to learn and practice these virtues. Please give me your ability to speak with discernment and prudence; I want to persuade others to come to a saving knowledge of you.

I dedicate myself in submission to the Holy Spirit to develop fruit in me. As I pray, study the Bible, and trust in God's power, I will receive and display gentleness, patience, kindness, and all spiritual gifts given to me for his glory. As I live in a way that shows the evidence of Christ in me, it will result in others seeing Jesus through me.

Peaceful Thoughts

You will keep in perfect peace
those whose minds are steadfast,
because they trust in you.

ISAIAH 26:3 NIV

Lord, I want to bring every thought I have captive to you. I want to rid my mind of the unlovely things that can linger in it. I confess the content that bombards my brain is often my fault. I choose most of what my eyes see and what my ears hear. I don't always make the best decisions about entertainment, and that can lead to ungodly thoughts that swirl for days. Even the evening news can taint my attitude and determine my mood.

From now on, I want to allow only what is pure and right in your sight to enter my mind. I ask for your strength and wisdom to make choices that honor you and bring me peace.

When I keep track of my thoughts, discerning what is pure and removing what is offensive to God, I experience his peace. I will trust the nudging of the Spirit and not expose myself to certain movies and music. I will keep a close eye on my mind to control what enters it. Then I will be able to say: "It is well with my soul."

Always Faithful

Trust in the Lord always,
for the Lord God is the eternal Rock.

ISAIAH 26:4 NLT

God, it can be hard to know who to trust. I have been hurt many times by people who promise but don't deliver. I have been disappointed when a confidence has been broken and secrets shared. I have felt let down when I depended on another's support, and they shrank back.

I am so thankful to know, beyond any doubt, that you are always trustworthy. You are my strength when I have none. You are my deliverer when I have no way out. You are the truth that I stand on. You are with me every minute of every day, and you will carry me victoriously from this life to the next. You alone are always faithful.

I declare that I know, belong to, and entrust every breath to the one true God. I know that my salvation is secure in Jesus Christ; I am certain of whom I believe. I have no reason to fear today or the future, for God has been and forever will be my security. He goes before me and prepares the way, and it is always good.

No Fear

The LORD is my light and my salvation—
whom shall I fear?
The LORD is the stronghold of my life—
of whom shall I be afraid?

PSALM 27:1 NIV

God, I can't always see my way, and it makes me afraid. In those times, I find myself feeling unprotected even though I know you are there. Why do I lose my faith so easily? I know I am human, but you have redeemed me. I should trust in that. Still, fear tempts me to doubt my security in you.

Please forgive me. Help me to believe all I have been given in Christ. I am chosen, forgiven, loved, and adopted as a child of God. I am sealed with the Holy Spirit, and I have fullness in Christ. I may approach the throne of God with freedom and confidence. Help me remember this and trust the truth of Jesus in me.

I have been made a new creation in Jesus. I have been saved by the power of his blood. In him, all fear is abolished, and the path he leads me on is full of light. Christ is the fortress that protects my life. My future is certain, and my existence with him is unending.

God My Father

Even if my father and mother abandon me,
the LORD will hold me close.

PSALM 27:10 NLT

Dear Father, we all have friends who are hurting. I want to bring a certain person before you today because they are struggling with their family. The issue might have started last week or many years ago. At times, they are at peace with this, but other times, they are tormented.

I now intercede on their behalf. Please hold them close. Remind them that you are the most faithful parent and family member. You are always there; you never leave. Whatever the reason, help them find peace and forgiveness. Heal them of their hurt. May they depend on you, their perfect heavenly Father.

God is my loving, trustworthy, and ever-present Father. I rejoice that I will never be abandoned, rejected, or uncared for; I am always protected by him. He desires to hold me close and call me his own. I am secure in the truth that I was made for God and by God. I will forever be with him.

Goodness of God

I would have despaired unless I had believed
that I would see the goodness of the Lord
In the land of the living.

PSALM 27:13 NASB

Jesus, you have once again brought me through a situation that I thought would do me in. I was in great distress until I turned to you and poured out my anguish and confusion. I was ready to give up, but I prayed, and you spoke. You reminded me of your goodness. You whispered a reminder of your promises. I heard you say, "Don't be anxious, my child. I've gone before you, and I've seen the beauty from the ashes."

My spirit lifted; my faith soared. I heard your answer and felt the resolve you brought. I rejoiced once again, for as always, you worked good out of evil and brought glory to your name.

God is righteous. All he does is for his glory and the benefit of those who love him. I trust in his plan and the great power that brings that plan to fruition. I know that regardless of how things might look, God is in control, and the victory that he brings is the answer to my prayers. I know, above all, that he is good.

Repentance and Restoration

If you cover up your sin you'll never do well.
But if you confess your sins and forsake them,
you will be kissed by mercy.
Guard your life carefully and be tender to God,
and you will experience his blessings.
But the stubborn, unyielding heart
will experience even greater evil

PROVERBS 28:13-14 TPT

Father, we both know there is this thing in my life that is a block. It's a guilty pleasure I have run to repeatedly. It's not good for me, and I have allowed it to enter my heart and control my actions. I have concealed this sin, and now it is making me sick inside.

I want to turn from this temptation that overshadows my relationship with you. Forgive me, gracious and merciful God. I am so thankful that when I repent, you cast my iniquities into the depths of the sea and remember them no more. Restore me and keep me from returning to anything that doesn't please you.

Because of God's goodness and grace, I have been forgiven. I believe that my sin is no more; my restoration in him is complete. I proclaim that I will keep a close watch over my heart and dedicate my whole being to my God. I have been transformed by the blood of Jesus. Sin and the grave have been defeated, and I live victoriously in Christ.

Ever-Present

> "Surely I am with you always,
> to the very end of the age."
>
> MATTHEW 28:20 NIV

Abba, there are times I feel lonely even in a room full of people. My spirit yearns for something and feels unfulfilled. As I search my heart, I realize it is due to a lack of time spent alone with you. Why do I get so distracted? Diversions take my attention off you. I should avoid them at all costs, but I often don't.

I am so thankful that even when I forget or tarry, you are there waiting for me. You have promised to be with me now and for eternity. When I feel alone, remind me to sit at your feet, receive your love, feel your comfort, and be completely renewed in your presence.

I declare that I serve the one true God of constant love, continual care, and perpetual presence. I know he desires my prayers and my heart. I believe that, more than anyone else in my life, he wants to be with me. That is a blessing I can't find words wonderful enough to describe.

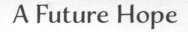

A Future Hope

"I know the plans I have for you," says the LORD.
"They are plans for good and not for disaster,
to give you a future and a hope."

JEREMIAH 29:11 NLT

Lord, when I look at my life, this world, and all the things that can go wrong, my head can't fully comprehend the potential downward spiral of it all. This can lead me to temptations of worry and fear and empty me of hope.

Then I hear that still, small voice. The one who is greater than anything in the world or in my life is in control. Your Word reveals that you created a plan before this universe even existed. That plan, through your Son, Jesus, is the promise of absolute hope for those who believe in him. There is guaranteed hope, the future is bright, and the end is victorious.

The Lord's plan is far more magnificent than my mind can conceive of. I believe there is nothing but hope, for he is sovereign. In his Word, he told me that we who are redeemed triumph in Christ. I will live in joy today, praising God for the future he has prepared for me.

Blessed Peace

The LORD gives strength to his people;
the LORD blesses his people with peace.

PSALM 29:11 NIV

Father, I can't imagine where I would be without you, but I know I'd be lost. I don't understand how anyone navigates life outside of salvation in you. I would be anxious more often than not. I would be powerless to maneuver the mishaps of everyday life or accomplish the dreams I desire in the absence of your intervention and favor. I know too well that without you, I can do nothing. Still, there are times I default to trying to do it on my own.

In those times of error, help me remember to repent and trust in the Almighty and all-sufficient God of all creation. You are more than able; you are waiting for me to step aside. I will watch you work wonders beyond my comprehension.

The Lord God is capable of the greatest acts and the most magnificent miracles. I receive the strength and perfect peace he graciously offers me, and I will forever worship him for his goodness. I praise him for his great generosity in providing everything I need and for his desire to continually bless me.

Faithful to Listen

"Then you will call on me and come and pray to me,
and I will listen to you."

JEREMIAH 29:12 NIV

Jesus, when I speak to others, I sometimes feel like they don't hear me. I have learned to watch for the glazed-over look in someone's eyes or the tendency for their heads to turn, looking elsewhere. It is then I know I have lost them, and my voice begins to self-consciously trail off.

Your Word assures me that you are always there to listen intently when I come to you. Thank you! I never have to wonder if you understand my deepest needs or hear my requests. You do more than hear me; you are eager to give me your full attention. There will never be a moment that you will miss my worship, my gratitude, or anything I have to ask of you.

Jesus is always available to hear my prayers, listen to my thoughts, and answer any need or question that I have. He will never reject me when I cry out to him. He will give heed with the utmost compassion. I will always have his ear, and he will be faithful to answer.

Greatest Treasure

"You will seek me and find me,
when you seek me with all your heart."

JEREMIAH 29:13 ESV

Father, I have often shopped or looked high and low for something I really wanted. When my heart is set on something, I go after it voraciously and don't give up. I understand from my experiences what that passion feels like. I know I need to seek and run after you in that way but with even more vigor. I want in my soul to desire you more than anything this life or world has to offer.

Forgive me for the times my desires have been terribly out of balance and not in your favor. Please keep me constantly aware of the blessing, the joy, and the reward of diligently seeking you and finding you.

My Savior God is the greatest treasure I could ever yearn for, pursue, and gain. I dedicate my heart in full to learn more about him, spend more time with him, and search for him with all my devotion. I know that when I place you as my ultimate priority, I will truly experience the abundant life you intend for me.

Child of the King

See how very much our Father loves us,
for he calls us his children,
and that is what we are!

1 JOHN 3:1 NLT

Father, when I consider your majesty and the magnitude of who you are, I feel so insignificant. When you look at me, you still see someone worth dying for. I am humbled and amazed by the grandeur of your affection for me. You call me your child, and I have been adopted through the blood of Christ.

This makes me speechless and yet moves me to shout for joy and praise. I desire nothing more than for you to guide me with your fatherly wisdom. When I am secure and believe in faith that I am sealed as your child forevermore, nothing in this life can dampen the overwhelming sense of my security and belonging. I am truly yours.

I am a child of the all-powerful God, and he is my Father. I am saved by the one true King. I rejoice in the heavenly royalty that is mine because of his mercy, grace, and love. I proclaim that I will always be his and he will always be mine. For eternity, I belong to the family of God.

Made for Eternity

God has made everything beautiful for its own time.
He has planted eternity in the human heart,
but even so, people cannot see the whole scope
of God's work from beginning to end.

ECCLESIASTES 3:11 NLT

Father, as the Creator of the universe, you made the miraculous materialize. In your perfect timing, you called into being sun and moon, sea and land, plants and animals, and finally, in your own image, man. Every morning, you give me breath. You cause the sun to rise to bring warmth to my being. In all this goodness, satisfaction can still remain out of reach. What do I long for?

When I read your Word, it brings clarity. Eternity. You have sown immortality in my soul. You have devised plans and purposes I don't fully comprehend. However, I am convinced that even though this world is my life's home, I won't be completely fulfilled until I live forevermore in your presence.

The Creator of all specifically made me to be in communion and exist forever with him. I know that this world and all it contains will never be enough, and it will pass away. I proclaim that I will live with joyful expectation and at peace, for I am assured that one day, I will live in God's kingdom where my days will never end.

July

He will answer
the prayers of the needy;
he will not reject
their prayers.

PSALM 102:17 NCV

Confidence in Prayer

Because of Christ and our faith in him, we can now come boldly and confidently into God's presence.

EPHESIANS 3:12 NLT

Father, I come before you in humility but also in the power of your Holy Spirit. In your Word, you say I will have what I ask of you if I ask with the right motives. Help me check my heart as I pour out a certain important request to you. I can't see my way out, and I don't know what to do. I need your wisdom; I need your intervention.

I am grateful that I don't have to walk this life alone. I don't struggle to find the answers on my own or suffer the eternal consequences of my poor choices. Through Christ, I know you will show me your way and make my paths straight.

When I come to God in prayer, he will hear me and answer. I will come courageously and with certainty, the veil torn away through the sacrifice of the Son. I enter his presence trusting I will be heard. My God will respond. I will have what I ask of him because of his great faithfulness.

Spiritual Family

I bow in prayer before the Father from whom every family in heaven and on earth gets its true name.

EPHESIANS 3:14-15 NCV

Father, because of your great salvation and my adoption as your child, I never have to wonder to whom I belong. You made every single human life in your image, and that is evidence that you want your created beings to be one big family.

I am sadly aware of so many that have rejected you. I kneel before you and petition for those in my life who have said no to your saving grace. May they turn to you and understand the magnitude of your love for them. I pray that those who receive your Son will experience the joy of Christ dwelling in their hearts and grow their faith in the power of your Holy Spirit. Please give me boldness and urgency to share your great plan of salvation.

Jesus sacrificed his life so I could be redeemed and live eternally with him. I declare that because of his great salvation, I can't keep quiet! I must share and fulfill the great commission. I commit to pray for those in my life who don't know Christ and ask for opportunities to speak truth that will lead them to repentance.

Holy Spirit Strength

I pray that from his glorious, unlimited resources he will empower you with inner strength through his Spirit.

EPHESIANS 3:16 NLT

Father, I have hit an impenetrable wall. I am overwhelmed and tired. I have over-committed myself. I know that your Word says when I am weak, you are strong. I believe that statement to be absolute truth, and I call on your endless supply of power to give me strength, lift me, and equip me. Please fill me with your Holy Spirit and enable me to accomplish all you have set before me.

I also ask that you give me peaceful and restorative sleep when I lay down at night. As I wake to a new day, renew me, ready me, and fill me with passion and purpose for your glorious kingdom.

I never have to accomplish anything on my own. I serve a God with whom all things are possible! I declare that he has given me everything I need in Christ. His spiritual gifts and boldness empower me to live with the single determination of furthering his gospel and bringing others to salvation. The unimaginable becomes achievable because of Jesus.

Greatest Provision

"God so loved the world that He gave His only begotten Son, that whoever believes in Him should not perish but have everlasting life."

JOHN 3:16 NKJV

Lord, what tremendous love that you would devise such a great salvation! What enormous sacrifice to give your only Son for a sinner such as me. I desire to speak freely and urgently to all I meet and tell them not to tarry, for now is the day of salvation. If they see with their hearts and believe that your desire for them is so immense, you allowed your only Son to carry their sin, then they could be saved. Their eternity hangs in the balance.

I know you want all to repent. Help me be ready with an answer for anyone who is open to listening. Thank you for this time of grace where all who believe in you can come. I pray for opportunities to be faithful to share the gospel.

Jesus is all I need to be saved. I believe that his death on the cross was out of his monumental love for every person who has or will ever live. I believe that through the power of the Holy Spirit, I will proclaim the truth of the cross to all who will listen.

Spirit of the Lord

The Lord is the Spirit,
and wherever the Spirit of the Lord is,
there is freedom.

2 CORINTHIANS 3:17 NLT

Dear Lord, you are like the wind that makes leaves whisper. What stirs the foliage is invisible to the naked eye, yet its power is intensely evident. Isn't this how it is with your Spirit? The ability of your holy advocate to be everywhere, move without being seen, and accomplish all things on the behalf of those who love you is amazing. It gives me confidence in the privileges I have in you.

I am empowered and free with the assurance that I have a comforter, companion, and encourager. As your Spirit moves to convict the world of its sin and righteousness, please help draw many to salvation.

I have received forgiveness and eternal life because I believe in Jesus, the only way, truth, and life. I admit joyfully that I am free from the wages of sin and death. I live unencumbered and unafraid, for I know the future and who holds it.

Wisdom of God

The wisdom that comes from God is first of all pure,
then peaceful, gentle, and easy to please. This wisdom
is always ready to help those who are troubled and to
do good for others. It is always fair and honest.

JAMES 3:17 NCV

God, I am thankful for the truth and insight of your Word.
Scripture invites me to ask for wisdom and assures me that
if I ask in faith, I will receive it. Lord, I realize that without
your guidance, my underlying motives for the decisions
and actions I choose in life are often outside of your will
for me. I confess that sometimes I run ahead of you while
trying to resolve my problems on my own.

I desire the results of today's verse. I want my life to exhibit
peace, gentleness, service, and honesty, but it is clear I can't
accomplish that without you. Please give me prudence
and discernment. Send a red flag to rise in my spirit when I
choose to take my own path instead of relying on you.

*In faith, I now request wisdom. I know I will receive what
I have asked of the Lord. I believe that his Word is always
trustworthy. I will look for the evidence of his knowledge
and direction in my life with the knowledge that he has
already answered my prayer.*

No Condemnation

"God did not send his Son into the world to condemn
the world, but to save the world through him."

JOHN 3:17 NIV

Lord, there is a cacophony of judgment throughout this
world. Ostracizing people because of their beliefs or
opinions has become the overriding pastime of our society.
I often hesitate to say what I think, afraid of conflict or
rejection, and I know others feel this way too.

I am thankful that I can say anything to you, my heavenly
Father, with confidence and without fear of being
turned away. You are the epitome of acceptance and
unconditional affection. Your greatest concern is that all
might understand the magnitude of your love and come
to repentance. I don't have to fear reproach from you or
anyone else; I can freely experience the greatest love of all
because of your crucified and risen Son.

*I never need to fear condemnation because I trust and love
my Savior. My present and my future is certain. Because
of the cross, I will not face judgment. I am saved now and
for eternity because of his outrageously generous gift of
salvation.*

Mighty Warrior Song

The LORD your God is with you,
the Mighty Warrior who saves.
He will take great delight in you;
in his love he will no longer rebuke you,
but will rejoice over you with singing.

ZEPHANIAH 3:17 NIV

Lord Almighty, the juxtaposition of you as mighty warrior and gentle singer is both baffling and absolutely thrilling. The greatest being of all time is triumphantly protective of me and tenderly adoring. It is the ultimate romance.

It is hard to comprehend that I, a creature of dust, am worth so much to you that you would sacrifice your only Son on my behalf. When it is your will, you grant grace and withhold rebuke from me, replacing it with your glorious voice of joyful song. May I grow to understand the depth, width, and expanse of your devotion; it is a love that could only be given from the heart of my heavenly Father, the Creator and ruler of all.

I declare that the Lord is my Savior, my deliverer, and the one who loves me. He vocalizes his tender love to me in marvelous power and passionate devotion. There is nothing he can't do, and everything he does is performed in his perfect will and for the good of his people.

Making Peace

The seed whose fruit is righteousness is sown in peace
by those who make peace.

JAMES 3:18 NASB

God, I have noticed that when my actions are formed out
of impure motives, nothing good results. I might feel I have
succeeded temporarily, but eventually the truth wins out.
The error of my impetuous ways is revealed and sabotages
any possible positive fruit.

Forgive me when I choose my stubborn, self-centered
ways over your wise and perfect plans. Draw me to seek
you and your leading. Help me listen for your instructive
voice and follow with obedience so the outcome is good in
your sight. I want to live in tranquility as a peacemaker who
is upright and focused on pleasing my holy Father. Make
me an ambassador for Christ who acts righteously and
spreads the fragrance of Jesus everywhere I go.

*God's ways are higher than mine and are guaranteed to
have the most ideal outcome. He sees what I can't, good
and bad; he will lead me in the everlasting way. I will pursue
your course for all my days so I may leave a legacy as a
peacemaking child of God.*

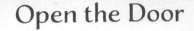
Open the Door

"Look! I stand at the door and knock.
If you hear my voice and open the door, I will come in,
and we will share a meal together as friends."

REVELATION 3:20 NLT

Jesus, I choose to invite you into every minute of my
life today. I want to do my best to please you, but I have
moments when I forget you are there. I can get overwhelmed
with the activities of the day and react in a way that is not
becoming of a child of God. I am thankful that when that
happens, you don't excuse yourself because of my bad
behavior. You kindly call me to repent. You lead me right
back into relationship with you, and we walk together as I
bask in your forgiveness and unconditional love.

Please make my heart your home. When it is desperately in
need of a deep cleaning, I know you will compassionately
nudge me. Restoring my connection with you is only a
confession away.

*My Savior is always with me, and I am never out of his sight.
His tender loving care is my constant companion. I declare
that I want him with me every second and over every
aspect of my life. I am fully his and his alone.*

God's Power

With God's power working in us, God can do much, much more than anything we can ask or imagine.

EPHESIANS 3:20 NCV

Father, according to your Word, the power available to me is far greater than I can comprehend. Still, it is real, and it is mine. Ephesians 1:19-20 says that this power is the same power that raised Jesus from the dead. This is so hard to fathom, but I must believe and act upon it. This removes all limitations and grants me the ability to do all things through you.

I must think bigger. I want my faith to stretch to the point that it can accept and utilize this omnipotent strength. That is your gift and your will for me. To doubt it or leave it unused would make me a lazy servant, so help me step into every aspect of authority you have given me in Christ.

God gave me a dynamic gift in allowing me to access the greatness of his power. I am astounded that he would choose me, yet he has not only made me his, he also works in me with the very power that belongs to him. He makes all things possible.

Glorious Bodies

He will take our weak mortal bodies and change them
into glorious bodies like his own, using the same power
with which he will bring everything under his control.

PHILIPPIANS 3:21 NLT

Oh Father, I get so weary from the aches, pains, and
stresses that everyday life places on me. I get distressed
about how broken the world around me is. I know you have
allowed free will at this point in history, yet I crave the day
when all will bow the knee to you. Everything will be under
your dominion.

I am grateful for your present grace which beckons all to
repentance, but I yearn for the new heaven and new earth
where we will dwell with you in bodies that no longer break
down. I pray the world will realize that today is the day of
salvation. I desperately want as many as possible to come
to you, but I also want you to return soon.

*I believe a day is coming, hopefully soon, when the bride of
Christ will be called home to be with the Lord for eternity.
What a glorious day that will be! I long to be with my God
in the beauty of his heavenly kingdom.*

Morning Mercies

The steadfast love of the Lord never ceases;
his mercies never come to an end;
they are new every morning;
great is your faithfulness.

LAMENTATIONS 3:22-23 ESV

Father, I praise you! When I awake every morning, not only do I know that I have begun another day surrounded by your presence, but I also know your limitless mercies toward me are brand new. Your trustworthiness is constant. I am comforted by the knowledge that you will always be with me in both life and death. There is nowhere I go that you do not accompany me, and nothing can separate us. Your affection for me is grander than my finite understanding could ever grasp, and it never ends.

What amazing love this is! I could never earn or deserve it, yet you freely offer it to me at the great cost and sacrifice of your Son. I am humbled beyond words. I thank you with all I am and surrender to your good and perfect will.

I know God in all his goodness, faithfulness, and power. This world doesn't understand how kind and compassionate he is; they don't know that his character is defined by love and mercy. I promise to be more aware of telling others exactly how wonderful my God is.

Trusting in the Cross

We are made right with God by placing our faith in Jesus Christ. And this is true for everyone who believes, no matter who we are. For everyone has sinned; we all fall short of God's glorious standard.

ROMANS 3:22-23 NLT

Jesus, I don't even want to consider what my fate would be without you. I am so thankful that you gave your life for a sinner such as myself. You were perfect, and I lived in disobedience to you. Because of your enormous love, you placed yourself in harm's way, suffering unthinkable torture and a horrific death. That death should have been mine. You gave me everything. All you ask is that I believe; that belief makes me right in your sight.

This truth is excused away by many who think it too simple, but for me, it constitutes an act that is undoubtedly the most beautiful sacrifice of all time. I admit with all my heart that I have fallen far short of your standards. I am dependent on the cross, and I trust my Savior.

I declare that because of the death and resurrection of my Savior and Lord, I have assurance and hope in the knowledge that I have been forgiven. He has discarded my filthy rags and made me righteous in Christ. I will rejoice!

Working for God

Whatever you do, work heartily, as for the Lord
and not for men, knowing that from the Lord
you will receive the inheritance as your reward.
You are serving the Lord Christ.

COLOSSIANS 3:23-24 ESV

Lord, when it comes to my job, my home life, and my
activities, I find that I am often performing to please a
person or myself. I try to tell myself I am doing it for you,
but that's just not the case. Your Word calls me to work
and serve you first and foremost, and this starts a debate
in my head. How do I do everything for you? How I will
ever be able to measure up?

Then I remember: you are not looking at the physical or
mental force behind my efforts, but, rather, the motive
of my heart. You are not calculating results. You reward
my surrender, my faith, and my commitment. Help me
remember that I am accountable to you alone and to
give you all I am. I know any task I approach is achievable
because you are doing it through me.

*From this day forward I will make a concentrated effort
to remember that I work for Christ, his kingdom, and the
furthering of the gospel. His approval is all I need or will seek.*

Sweet Sleep

When you lie down, you will not be afraid;
when you lie down, your sleep will be sweet.

PROVERBS 3:24 NIV

Father, you know that I struggle with sleep. When I lay down, the enemy of my mind sets up a racket. Hey, it whispers. Remember this problem? This pile of too many commitments? That friend who is annoyed with you? That sin you are hiding? I often let the mental torment go on too long before I tell Satan to take a hike. I do this by recalling your presence and your protection. I focus on the truth of today's verse; you want me to lie down and sleep calmly.

Fear should never interrupt my rest. You are with me while I dream, watching over me and sending a night that restores and rejuvenates. Thank you for being Jehovah Shammah, "The Lord Is There." You, my God, will never leave me.

From now on, I will immediately thrust away any attack from my mind and take my captive thoughts to the Lord's throne. I rejoice that when I climb in bed, I can be certain that his watchful eyes are on me. His desire is for my peaceful rest.

Wait Quietly

The LORD is good to those who depend on him,
to those who search for him.
So it is good to wait quietly
for salvation from the LORD.

LAMENTATIONS 3:25-26 NLT

Life is full of surprises, Father. I find solace in the fact that I can depend on you in good times and bad. I am comforted by the truth that regardless of what difficulty I face, I will find you if I seek you. I rejoice that your every intent is for my good. When I have something to celebrate, you are smiling and singing over me.

On those occasions when I can't figure out my next step, I will sit silently by your feet. I know I will hear your voice telling me to go to the right or the left. You assure me you have gone ahead and know all my ways. There is confidence in staying connected to the vine in faith and assurance.

I will not go my own way. I will follow my heavenly Father's lead in everything. I declare that he knows best. He is always working in unseen places on my behalf, and all I need to do is wait and trust. All my dependence is on him and his good and perfect will for me.

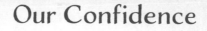

Our Confidence

The Lord will be your confidence
and will keep your foot from being caught.

PROVERBS 3:26 ESV

Sometimes, Lord, I feel so brave. Other times, I'm afraid of my own shadow. I don't understand how I can switch so quickly between confidence and timidity. It is most likely a case of either too much pride or too much fear. I want to repent of both, lean on you, and trust in faith that you are my confidence.

Help me remember that you are the mighty warrior who saved me. You will continue to protect me until you call me to my heavenly home. You designed my destiny, and I can be assured that my path is clear, and my footing is sure. You will be faithful to fulfill your good and perfect will for my life here and into eternity.

I know that nothing is impossible with the Lord; I can do all things through Christ. I declare that my salvation is sure. My courage comes from him, and I am covered and safe in the shadow of his wings. I believe his promise that with him by my side, I am always secure.

My Deliverer

The Lord is faithful;
he will strengthen you
and guard you from the evil one.

2 THESSALONIANS 3:3 NLT

Lord, you reign over all. There is none greater than you. Even when the enemy plans a vicious attack, his attempts are dismal failures compared to your faithfulness and fortitude. You are sovereign, and you rule over all creation. You are trustworthy and always on my side. There is no weapon formed against me that can stand, no evil scheme of Satan that can prevail. You are my strength and my shield, and you impart to me the boldness to defeat evil.

I am thankful that your Word is the wisdom lighting my path. When I act in obedience, there is no sense to fear and every reason to be certain of victory. Nothing can ever harm me, for you are my deliverer. There is no one more powerful than you.

I serve the one true God who is far above all in wisdom, knowledge, discernment, and power. He is Creator, Savior, defender, and the lover of my soul. I know I am guarded from all harm, destined to be victorious and endlessly covered by his tender, everlasting love.

Steady Armor

Lord, you are my shield,
my wonderful God who gives me courage.

PSALM 3:3 NCV

Father, I am so sorry for the times I forget your powerful presence with me. When difficult situations arise, they throw me into an anxious cycle where fear becomes my downfall. If I made the problem, it only makes matters worse when I try to defend myself and end up in even deeper trouble. I am painfully aware that these cycles lead only to stress, worry, and faulty strategies.

I confess to not trusting you as my deliverer. I often don't bring my crisis directly to you in faith. Help me to remember that if I seek you, you will give me all I need. I know you will guide me and give me the tenacity to face any trial. You are my safe and steady armor.

God is my King, my defender, and the power that protects and leads me. I declare that my desire is to look to him before I even begin to contemplate a resolution to my issues. I know he has all the answers. When I place myself in his hands, I am safe.

Never Abandoned

No one is abandoned by the Lord forever.
Though he brings grief, he also shows compassion
because of the greatness of his unfailing love.

LAMENTATIONS 3:31-32 NLT

Father, I know that you will never allow anything to come into my life that is not ultimately for my good, but right now I am hurting. I sometimes wonder why it must be this way. Still, I know your character. You are kind, caring, and merciful. I am certain you will never abandon me and will always love me, but I just don't understand why this life has so much pain.

I am thankful that a day will come when you erase all my tears; you have promised it. Misery will never again affect me. I pray you will hasten the time when I will be transformed to a perfect body and reside in paradise with you forever.

Even though I may not understand this difficult time, I know the Lord is carrying me through it. I believe that he has a purpose for me. His plans are to prosper me, not to harm me. I am thankful that even when I fall into discouragement and become unfaithful, God remains faithful. My flesh may fail, but he will always carry me through to victory.

He Equips Us

We are not saying that we can do this work ourselves. It is God who makes us able to do all that we do.

2 CORINTHIANS 3:5 NCV

Father, the thought of taking on a new task in ministry is so exciting. I am humbled by the fact that you want to use me. Then I think of all the work and talent the venture will entail, and I start to worry. I wonder whether I am enough for the job.

When I am fretting over a commitment I'm about to make, lead me to this verse. What a beautiful reminder that I am just the vessel; you are the power that works through me. I gain confidence knowing that all things are possible with you and that you have promised to be with me and equip me. I will move forward knowing that I can do everything through you.

The Lord God Almighty is all-powerful and all-sufficient. In Christ, he has given me everything I need to fulfill his will. I will proceed with boldness knowing that he is the one who gives abilities and brings results. I commit to his service knowing that he will accomplish his plan.

Dependence

Trust the LORD with all your heart,
and don't depend on your own understanding.
Remember the LORD in all you do,
and he will give you success.

PROVERBS 3:5-6 NCV

Father, I know you and trust you completely, so why do I doubt when I think I have heard your voice's direction? I ask for your wise guidance, and then I waver. With my limited insight, I start to wonder if I'd really heard you.

Please help me recognize your voice immediately and act upon your counsel. I know that if I go my own way, I will most assuredly fail, but the truth of your Word says if I listen and obey, you will grant me success. I don't want to go anywhere or do anything that is not your will. Please give me discernment and reverence when it comes to following your lead. Help me depend solely on you.

Heavenly Father, I declare with all my heart that, from this day forward, I will sit at my Father's feet, listen intently for his voice, and depend solely on his leading in my life. I desire to be blessed by him, and I want to honor him in everything I do. I will trust him with my whole heart and surrender to all he asks of me.

Filled and Renewed

He saved us through the washing of rebirth and renewal by the Holy Spirit, whom he poured out on us generously through Jesus Christ our Savior, so that, having been justified by his grace, we might become heirs having the hope of eternal life.

TITUS 3:5-7 NIV

Father, I am overwhelmed with great joy and gratitude because you have saved me. I could do nothing in my own strength to be redeemed; it is only by your grace that I have been forgiven and transformed. This is too grand for me to fully comprehend, but I believe. When I consider the fact that you chose me first and adopted me as your child, it is too wonderful for words.

I have been made clean through the refreshing flow of the blood of Christ. I belong to you. I have all I could ever desire and far more than I could ever need. Everything in this world pales in comparison to the greatest love of all and the hope of living with you throughout eternity.

I have been made new through the cross of Christ and the filling of his Holy Spirit. I know that he has never withheld anything good from me. He has always given me his very best. I receive his generous justification by his grace, and I have found my salvation and identity in Jesus.

Battle Blessings

Do not repay evil for evil or abuse for abuse;
but, on the contrary, repay with a blessing.
It is for this that you were called—
that you might inherit a blessing.

1 PETER 3:9 NRSV

Lord, sometimes your ways are difficult to adhere to. When I get hurt by another or someone harms one of my loved ones, I react internally and sometimes externally, and it is often not in a way that pleases you. My emotions rage at the insensitivity and cruelty of others. I don't want to respond this way, but I can't seem to restrain myself.

I need you desperately, not only to give me self-control but also to remind me that my battle is not against flesh and blood. When a situation arises, please help me to respond as you would. Help me to bless instead of curse. If I repay offense with kindness, I know it will honor you.

With the power of the Holy Spirit, I can react to any circumstance in a way that will point to God's goodness and love. Ephesians says that I have God's power, the same power he exerted when he raised Christ from the dead. I declare that I will use that ability fully when dealing with the misdeeds of others.

None Should Perish

The Lord is not slow to fulfill his promise as some count slowness, but is patient toward you, not wishing that any should perish, but that all should reach repentance.

2 PETER 3:9 ESV

Heavenly Father, you desire that all would to come to repentance, and it is evidence of the enormity of your love and kindness. The fact that you tarry because you are allowing as many as possible to choose to repent may be seen by some as delaying, but I view it as extravagant grace.

I pray that you would give me eyes to see those who are on the fence about giving their heart to you. I want to be bold in sharing the truth of your salvation. I ask that many who are aware of your love but have not yet given their lives to you will realize that today is the day. They can secure their position in eternity with you by believing in the name of your Son.

I declare that there is no other way and no other name by which we can be saved but that of Jesus Christ. I know that I have been given the great commission, and I have God's power to speak truth. I will look for those who don't know Jesus and share the truth of his saving grace.

Salvation and Strength

In repentance and rest is your salvation,
in quietness and trust is your strength.

ISAIAH 30:15 NIV

Father, I know that the only true way to salvation in Christ is believing that when I come to you, confess my sin, and turn from it, I am saved. Help me find rest from any doubt or questioning by trusting in your promises. I can find my security in you because I know that my redemption has been accomplished in the sacrifice of Jesus on the cross.

I am revived, renewed, and restored because you are faithful to your Word. You will fulfill the good work in me that you prepared in advance before I was even born. All my days are accounted for by you, and every single one will be completed. Once my days are through, I will enter eternity to be with you always. For that, I give you endless praise.

In his wisdom, our Father has provided everything we could ever need or hope for. I declare my salvation and eternity was provided by him. Without the Son, I would never be able to enter the triune God's presence. I rest in the absolute truth that there is nothing I can add, for Jesus took my place and paid my debt.

Graciously Just

The LORD waits to be gracious to you,
and therefore he exalts himself to show mercy to you.
For the LORD is a God of justice;
blessed are all those who wait for him.

ISAIAH 30:18 ESV

Father, I know that when I go astray, you are waiting for me to come to you and repent so you can graciously restore me. You aren't angry; you are merciful. You want me to rid myself of my sin and come close to you. You are a great and awesome God who is extravagantly loving. Sometimes, I would rather focus on that and conveniently forget that you are also a God of justice, especially when I am indulging in sin.

You won't turn a blind eye to my transgression, but you will forgive immediately when I ask. You bless me by inviting me into your presence and thoroughly cleansing me from my guilt. Thank you for being everything to me: the lover of my soul, my King, and my Redeemer.

I want to shout from the rooftops how gracious, compassionate, and amazing God is! I declare that he revealed his faithfulness, constant care, and overwhelming love by sending his Son in my place. I want the world to see him for who he really is. I will proclaim his goodness to all.

In His Timing

O Lᴏʀᴅ my God, I cried to you for help,
and you have healed me.

Psᴀʟᴍ 30:2 ᴇsᴠ

Father, I have experienced being worn and weary from months of struggle, long sleepless nights, and reoccurring mornings that bring no relief. I cried out to you, pouring out more tears that I thought I could produce. I admit I panicked at times when I didn't rest in you, but as always, you faithfully stayed with me and coaxed me to your presence. As I continued to seek you, I realized that you were constantly working through this difficult, painful time. There was never a moment that I or my situation escaped your mind.

I praise you for your mighty work! Your answer to my trial is more than I could imagine even asking for. You have brought healing and complete restoration, and I will praise you forevermore.

God is an all-powerful, faithful, brilliant, and miraculous God. I declare that I serve the Lord God Almighty who is healer, provider, the Good Shepherd, and my righteous and holy King. He is the God who never leaves me, and he always provides the best answers in his perfect timing.

The Right Path

When you turn to the right or when you turn to the left,
your ears shall hear a word behind you, saying,
"This is the way; walk in it."

ISAIAH 30:21 NRSV

Precious Father, I can't express how grateful I am for your loving guidance. I was stressed and confused about what to do and which way to go. I am sorry that, at the onset, I tried to decipher it on my own. Unfortunately, I still default to going my own way at times, and I prayerfully ask that you continue to work on me in that area.

I don't want to waste any time in life getting off the track that leads where you want to send me. You have a plan, and it is always the best plan. I am thankful that you drew me to yourself and gently whispered, "Not that way. Take this way." I will follow your will, not mine, for my good and for your kingdom.

I am so grateful that I serve the one true God who is all-powerful and deeply personal. He rules the universe, yet he is concerned with every hair on my head. I affirm that there is no direction I want to go other than the one he has ordained for me. I declare that I will follow the Lord all my days.

Lavishing Goodness

How great is the goodness
you have stored up for those who fear you.
You lavish it on those who come to you for protection,
blessing them before the watching world.

PSALM 31:19 NLT

Father, when I imagine your storehouse filled with good blessings for those who revere you, and how generously you want to pour them out, it makes me giddy. I'm a child that respects you and is in awe of you. Because of that, you want to bless me exponentially.

I am humbled and privileged to be yours. I know that you desire all to come to repentance and receive the forgiveness that brings eternal security in Christ. You do good in full view of the world so all can see how you bless and protect those who love you. You don't do this to boast but to bring as many as possible to you. You want to save the world, and you love and provide the same enormous grace to all you have created.

God is great, always good, and incredibly benevolent to those who love him. He reveals his goodness so the universe can see how great his love is for his creation. I declare that no eye has seen, and no mind can conceive, what the Lord has prepared for those who love him.

August

I am praying to you
because I know you
will answer, O God.
Bend down and
listen as I pray.

PSALM 17:6 NLT

Satisfying Refreshment

"I will refresh the weary
and satisfy the faint."

JEREMIAH 31:25 NIV

Father, what a comfort and a joy to know that when I am on my last leg, you are there to strengthen me. Whether it is physical exhaustion or weariness from crying too many tears, your remedy is healing and restorative. However, I sometimes tarry, wallowing in my tired state and feeling a bit too sorry for myself.

Help me bypass the pity party and come to you immediately, the fountain of life, the one who makes all things new. I know I will find rest and experience satisfying revival because my heavenly Father is the one doing the good work in me. Thank you for being my perfectly wise and all-knowing Savior; you always give me exactly what I need.

My heavenly Father has infinite wisdom, limitless power, and tender love for me. I acknowledge that he is the God of the universe. Still, he looks upon me, his lowly servant, and cares for my weariness. I declare that I will run to him with joyful expectation for his compassionate healing.

The Greatest Love

"I have loved you with an everlasting love;
I have drawn you with unfailing kindness."

JEREMIAH 31:3 NIV

Lord, you know that in the depths of my heart, my utmost cry is to be known, understood, and loved. My craving for all-encompassing affection is voracious; without its fulfillment, my soul would be empty. You fill that hole. You, the God of all creation, loved me first. That is humbling and exhilarating!

Before I even had a thought of you, I was already destined to be yours. You called me out of darkness into your glorious light with your voice of compassion. You chose me and promised that if I believed in your name, I would dwell in your presence for eternity. You amaze me with your abundant goodness. I am grateful to belong to you and experience your love, the greatest love of all.

There is none like the Lord God Almighty. His love seems too good to be true, yet it is authentic. He has blessed me with this bountiful love. I will seek him with every ounce of my being. I will live filled with his Spirit; I will exist for his glory.

He Goes before Me

The LORD himself will go before you.
He will be with you;
he will not leave you or forget you.
Don't be afraid and don't worry.

DEUTERONOMY 31:8 NCV

In times past, Father, I have thought that I needed you, but it was never like this. I don't think I can even take my next breath, let alone another step, unless you do it. I am paralyzed by what I know is coming and what I must do to walk through it. It's staggering, and I can't stand the thought of it.

I praise you, for you have already gone ahead of me. You see where I'm going even though I'm walking in the dark, frightened of what I will run into. Then I remember you, and I am encouraged to know you are there. You will not leave me alone. There is no need for concern, for the one who created me and designed my destiny knows the way. He will guide me there safely.

I declare, before all heaven, that there has never been a single second when my Lord's faithful care has not gone before me and surrounded me. I affirm that I will follow him with complete confidence all the days of my life.

Righteousness of God

The fruit of that righteousness will be peace;
its effect will be quietness and confidence forever.

ISAIAH 32:17 NIV

Father, although I had no righteousness of my own, I have become your righteousness through Jesus Christ. All I had to offer was filthy rags, a broken-down life of sin that I could never overcome on my own. I was spiritually dead, but you saw a diamond in the rough. You looked at me and saw what the sacrifice of your Son had accomplished. His salvation has made me right with you, and now I have confidence that I am forgiven. One day, when I leave this earth, I will live with you and worship you endlessly.

I am overflowing with joy as I sit quietly at your feet. I relish every minute in your presence, listening for your still small voice that sweetly speaks of your great love for me. Thank you for this righteousness.

In the quietness of this moment with my Father, I would love nothing more than to shout from the rooftops of his goodness. I declare that in Christ alone is peace, assurance, and the hope of eternity.

A House of Peace

"My people will live free from worry in secure,
quiet homes of peace."

Isaiah 32:18 TPT

Father, I live in a world that is bursting at the seams with stress and fear of the unknown. So much is going, and could go, wrong, and you can see the worry on people's faces. I miss the smiles of strangers in a time when things were gentler and not so complicated. I do find respite in being in your sanctuary with other believers, but I confess I have not been thoroughly involved in my church body.

I am craving fellowship. I know in your house I will find loving support, hope, and peace. The church holds my spiritual family, and I want to serve them, do life with them, and never neglect them. It is where I belong and where I thrive. Help me throw off the temptation of a lazy Sunday morning and show up to worship with my brothers and sisters in Christ.

I belong to the Father, and I have a big, beautiful family in Christ. I declare that no catastrophic world events can cause me concern because I know my future with him. I affirm that I have peace and live with complete confidence in his promises.

Great Defender

You are my hiding place;
you protect me from trouble.
You surround me with songs of victory.

PSALM 32:7 NLT

Father, I remember having nightmares as a child that would send me under the covers. I recall noises in the night that would make me bolt out of bed and hide underneath it. My mind was filled with monsters, and I would shut my eyes tightly and try to think of something pretty.

I can almost feel the warmth that came over me as I huddled there, the reassurance that flooded my young mind: my great defender was near. Words and melodies of songs I sang in Sunday school would strengthen me. Eventually, I would come out of hiding because I was reassured by you, my protector, the one who never takes his eyes off me. I thank you that you have never, nor will you ever, leave me. I am yours forever.

I have a heavenly Father who adores and protects me. I declare that through Jesus, I have great worth. God highly values me as his child. He will never allow anything in my life that is not of his will, and I can look forward to days filled with peace and joy.

Needed Counsel

I will instruct you and teach you
in the way you should go;
I will counsel you with my loving eye on you.

PSALM 32:8 NIV

Father, I must confess that I have done it again. You know my propensity to go my own way. I know it is foolish, and I can't understand why I continue to do what pleases me instead of what pleases you. It never turns out well, and the pleasurable parts last only a nanosecond before my guilt kicks in. I want to turn and repent, but I am scared that I will return to that sin. Until now, I have been avoiding the conversation.

Please teach me. If I don't get it, compassionately correct me until I do. I know you love me and only discipline me for my own good. I need your counsel, and I want to follow you all the days of my life. I am so thankful that you don't leave me as I am. Your desire is to transform me into the image of your Son.

I am done going my own way. I affirm that I have no power to do that on my own; I need the Spirit's wisdom and counsel constantly. He will always guide me.

Just What I Need

"My presence will go with you,
and I will give you rest."

Exodus 33:14 ESV

Lord, I am so thankful that you are my banner and that you always go before me. However, today is one of those days where I feel like I can't take another step. I am exhausted. Everywhere I turn, someone needs something from me, and I am drained.

I love it when you give me people to serve, but I really need relief right now. Will you please send someone to be that refreshment to me? I know you are always there ready to revive me and give me peace, but could I have someone with skin on right now? You understand my need for a human hug because you created our need for connection. Thank you in advance for whomever you are sending my way; I know you are faithful.

There is no greater God than my God! He understands my heartfelt desires and provides just what I need. He affirms his personal presence with me and also sends fellow Christians to me when I need someone to laugh or cry with. He loves and cares for me.

Hidden Treasures

"Call to me and I will answer you,
and will tell you great and hidden things
that you have not known."

JEREMIAH 33:3 ESV

My precious Lord, this verse has always beckoned me with great mystery and enticement. I want to run as fast as I can into your presence, call out to you, and be witness to marvelous things I have not yet been privy to. I try to imagine the magnificence of all those great, concealed treasures you desire to reveal.

Please tell me, Father. Here I am, ears attentive, listening intently to all you want to speak and share. I will sit here in your presence until I am satisfied with the sound of your voice and the manifestation of the knowledge you hold so dear. I desire to be your confidante, the one you entrust your insight to. Let me be the one who boldly shares the magnitude of how great and mighty you are.

I declare that God's knowledge and thoughts are far above and beyond mine. I can't begin to comprehend his understanding, but I desire to know the hidden nuggets of his wisdom. I believe that as I seek and find him, I will be invited to hear the greatest truths of all from God himself.

Trustworthy and True

The word of the LORD holds true,
and we can trust everything he does.

PSALM 33:4 NLT

Lord, there was a game I used to play with friends. Everyone had to guess if someone was telling the truth or not. For me, it became a powerful illustration. Although it was meant to be entertaining, I didn't like being lied to or tricked. Some of my friends were so convincing that I wondered if the words they spoke outside of game could be trusted. I know that I am not innocent in this myself. Many times, I have told a convenient white lie to avoid hurting someone's feelings or putting myself in an awkward position.

If I am questioning others, I should take a good hard look at myself first. Please magnify the twinge of guilt I feel when I am being less than honest; help me repent right away. I want to be trustworthy by following your example.

I will be on my guard, looking for and confessing immediately anything I say or do that is not truthful. I want to honor God. From this day forward, I affirm that I will check the motive of my heart regularly.

A Proper Fear

In that day he will be your sure foundation,
providing a rich store of salvation,
wisdom, and knowledge.
The fear of the LORD will be your treasure.

ISAIAH 33:6 NLT

Father, thank you for proper fear of you. This fear does not mean I need to be afraid of you; it means I must give you respect and reverence for your authority and the truth of your Word. I want a God-fearing attitude that leads to life full of wisdom and good fruit. This desire helps me turn from temptation, for only in obedience will I find peace.

I am thankful that your perfect love casts out any worry over judgment of my transgressions, for my sins were resolved and forgiven at the cross. I rejoice that I have been adopted by you and purified through salvation in Christ. I stand on the rock of Jesus knowing that my worth, which is of great value to you, is mine because of my risen Savior.

I stand in amazement of God's goodness and his unfathomable ways. I declare that he has not given me a spirit of fear but of power, love, and sound mind. My reverence for him is due to the enormous esteem I have for who he is.

Ready to Restore

The Lord is close to all
whose hearts are crushed by pain,
and he is always ready to restore the repentant one.

PSALM 34:18 TPT

God, I confess that I have been avoiding you. I want to please you, but then I fall into the same sin again. It pains me to know that I notice it less and less and as I build calluses around my own wrongdoing. I come to accept it and diminish in my mind the fact that it is sin.

Thank you for not ignoring my sin. You continue to prod me toward repentance. I am grateful that you never give up on me. You never stop helping me reach the destiny you have planned for my life. I am ashamed of my sin, but when I do come to you with a contrite heart, you lift up my head. When I confess, you are faithful and righteous to forgive me and restore me to relationship with you.

The Father is full of endless goodness. He will never reject me when I bring my filthy, ragged heart before him in repentance. I become pure, washed, and fully forgiven by his grace. I have been redeemed, and I can walk in the security of my salvation.

A Radiant Face

Those who look to him are radiant;
their faces are never covered with shame.

PSALM 34:5 NIV

Father, when I stand before you after confessing the condition of my heart, I am at that moment without sin, and I am filled with inexpressible joy. I smile because knowing that you are pleased with me is the best feeling. Even when I come to you tarnished with sin, your Word says that I don't need to feel covered with humiliation, for your abundant forgiveness is always available to me.

Regardless of my state, whether I present myself before you in confession or in praise and worship, I am accepted. What a compassionate and merciful heavenly Father you are! I am always at peace knowing that you will forever love me and receive me, for I am your very own.

I declare that today and every day is meant to be filled with rejoicing because of the Lord's goodness. Nothing I do can banish me from his presence. He is all I need; he is my everything. Because of that, my face is radiant!

My Good Refuge

O taste and see that the LORD is good;
happy are those who take refuge in him.

PSALM 34:8 NRSV

Father, there is no better place to be than in your presence. I am never safer than when I trust in and submit to your guidance and protection. On the occasions when I try to handle things alone or go my own way, I always end up distressed, confused, and often with unfortunate results.

Please lead me to never take matters into my own hands. When I remember who you are—all-powerful, ever-present, and always wise—in every act, I do my best to come under your sovereign will. When I surrender and stay in line with your leading, I find peace and contentment in realizing that all will be well because you are in control. I am so grateful that I never have to navigate this life alone. I have the wise and all-knowing God of creation to direct my path.

I am overjoyed because I have been the recipient of the Lord's perfect love and care. I proclaim that I serve a great and awesome God who is good in all he does. I know that his thoughts toward me are to prosper me, and for that, I praise him!

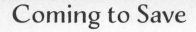

Coming to Save

Say to those with fearful hearts,
"Be strong, and do not fear,
for your God is coming to save you."

ISAIAH 35:4 NLT

Lord, there have been times in my life when attacks from the enemy paralyzed me with fear. I wanted so badly to be rescued, but I chose to wallow in my anxiety instead of handing the battle over to you so you could deliver me. The words from today's verse, "your God is coming to save you," truly resonate when I trust in you. I envision my powerful Savior riding in on a white horse to save me and destroying any weapon pointed in my direction. He drives back the black clouds and lets the sun of hope shine.

When the arrows furiously fly, help me find the courage to climb out of my desperate state directly into the safety of your loving arms. I will find my strength in you.

From this day forward, I want to run directly into my Lord's arms at the first sign of spiritual battle. I will not attempt to fight on my own; I will surrender to his saving grace. I declare that there is nowhere else to go but the strong and mighty protection of my Lord and Savior.

Faithfully Forbearing

You, O Lord, your mercy-seat love is limitless,
reaching higher than the highest heavens.
Your great faithfulness is so infinite,
stretching over the whole earth.

PSALM 36:5 TPT

Precious Lord, I come before your throne in confidence that I will receive your immeasurable compassion. You have always shown me divine favor that is inexhaustible. When I try to envision the height of your heaven, I can't imagine it. The fact that your kind forbearance reaches far beyond that distance fills me with gratitude.

You have been steadfast in your faithfulness toward me every day of my life. There has never been a time or a place that you have not been beside me, going before me to provide and prepare your very best for me. Your blessings are boundless, and all your children are the recipients. I reside in continual awe and wonder at the expanse of your enormous love for me and all you have created.

I declare that I am absolutely, thoroughly, and perfectly loved by my heavenly Father. I proclaim that I am now, and will forever be, covered by his protection, provision, and power. I know that he never takes his eyes off me. He never tires of guiding all my ways. I receive his mercy, grace, forgiveness, and blessings with a full heart of thankfulness.

Righteous Care

Your righteousness is like the mighty mountains,
your justice like the ocean depths.
You care for people and animals alike, O LORD.

PSALM 36:6 NLT

Heavenly Lord, I know that as the God of the universe, you are perfectly pure. All your ways are virtuous. Your power, wisdom, and integrity are far beyond the highest peak, and I tend to feel like a small speck. Your Word says we are like the flowers that bloom and then fall away.

Life is short. It passes like the wind, and all our days are numbered by you. You are ruler of all and almighty in your ways, yet your goodness and care toward me is gentle and birthed in the greatest love. Your affection even extends to my beloved pets. The entirety of what and who you are is almost incomprehensible, but I believe and am eternally grateful for the God you are. You are my omnipotent King, my Abba, my righteous Savior, and the lover of my soul.

I declare that the holy Lord God Almighty is the one true God: all-powerful, sovereign, and immutable. There is none greater than him. I rejoice that his extravagant love goes beyond the most tender father. I fully receive my royal position in Christ.

Flowing Fountain

To know you is to experience a flowing fountain,
drinking in your life, springing up to satisfy.
In your light we receive the light of revelation.

PSALM 36:9 TPT

Father, this verse makes me feel weightless. The absence
of stress allows me to soak up the light emanating from
you. I can almost taste the spiritual water you provide that
heals my entire being and gives assurance of my secure
salvation in you. Your illumination is endless and always
lends abundant brightness to my ways.

Existence in your Son affords me entrance to the promise
of forever in your presence. Your love and plan for me are
revealed in your perfect timing and performed by your
all-powerful hand. There is fullness in the depths of my
soul because of the provision of your everlasting love
and faithful plans for me. There is no greater delight than
drinking rich redemption from your life-giving fountain.

*Because I am forgiven and saved, transformed by Jesus'
death and resurrection, I will forever draw refreshment
from the Lord, the fountain of life. His sacrificial provision
has afforded me deliverance from destruction and brings
eternity with him. He is the light that illumines my way here
and into his heavenly kingdom.*

Humbly Rejoice

The humble of heart will inherit every promise
and enjoy abundant peace.

PSALM 37:11 TPT

Lord, I must admit that it really bothers me when
some individuals I know boast about their lives or their
possessions. I get angry, and it makes me want to steer
clear of them whenever I see them coming. I hadn't
identified why I react so strongly until I read this verse
today. Your Word reveals to me that I have a jealous heart. I
am tempted to brag about anything and everything just to
invade their airspace, but this steals my peace.

Please forgive me. Help me recognize when I am envious
and confess it. Help me humbly rejoice when others have
success. You alone fulfill what you have promised in my life.
I don't want to compare with others; I want to be grateful
for all you have promised and given me.

*I declare with all my being that God alone is great and
worthy of praise. The earth and all within it belong to him
alone. I understand fully that all good things come from
him. I will aim to rejoice for the blessings he brings to
others while remaining thankful for all he has provided me.*

Delightful Directions

The Lord directs the steps of the godly.
He delights in every detail of their lives.

PSALM 37:23 NLT

Lord, as I look back over my life, every single time I surrendered to your guidance, my path was blessed. I felt your smile and approval radiating around me. So why do I ever revert to trying to do things on my own? There are moments when I don't even realize I am jumping ahead without you. I start to think I am past this behavior and then I end up here, recognizing that I am repeating it again.

I humbly ask your forgiveness. Please whenever I step out on my own, tenderly derail me and pull me back. I want to walk in step with you so that my ways are pleasing, and my life is protected by your wise direction.

The Lord's knowledge and wisdom surpass that of any other. I am so thankful that he created his perfect plan for me out of his good and righteous will. I rejoice that when I submit, he finds pleasure in me. I declare that I will follow him in obedience all my days.

Holding Hands

Though they stumble, they will never fall,
for the LORD holds them by the hand.

PSALM 37:24 NLT

Great God, I am relieved that you have forgiven and
forgotten the sins that made me stumble in the past. I
don't have sufficient words to explain how grateful I am
that you have never deserted me even though I have done
things that deserve it. You have never given up on me, and
you watched over me even when I had chosen a dark road.

I committed my life to your Son many years ago, and
that has sealed me inside your loving protection. I wish I
wouldn't, but I know I will sin again. When I do tumble into
transgression, your guiding hand will lift me up and set me
back on the right path when I repent. I am so thankful for
that! You will hold my hand through this life continually and
at the end when you lead me into your eternal kingdom.

*God is my constant companion and gracious guide. I know
that I will be safe in all my ways with him taking the lead. I
rejoice in holding his hand as he fulfills his will in my life.*

Delight in Him

Take delight in the LORD,
and he will give you the desires of your heart.

PSALM 37:4 NIV

Father, I admit I could go a bit off the rails with this verse promising the desires of my heart. I might try to manipulate the emotions I have to be rewarded with a wanted result. I do take great pleasure in you, my Lord. I love you with my whole heart, but I can be greedy about things I mistakenly believe I am entitled to. That can contribute to attitudes that wrongfully affect the impulses I operate from.

I want to deny myself and follow you. You deserve my devotion filled with praise, truthfulness, and faithful obedience. You have given me everything I could ever need or want in Jesus Christ. I am exceedingly thankful and speak in all honesty when I say that you are the absolute delight of my life.

I declare that my precious heavenly Father is the light of my life, the lover of my soul, and the entirety of all I could ever desire. There is no one and nothing more wonderful than him, and I am thrilled to be able to rejoice in who he is. My Savior is my reward.

Following Footsteps

Commit your way to the LORD
trust in him, and he will act.

PSALM 37:5 ESV

Lord, I need your help. I have things coming at me that I can't handle, and I have no way of avoiding them. I want to depend on you in complete faith. I want to squash any stress that tries to divert my emotions and intellect from believing that you've got this. I know you are trustworthy and have always been faithful, so why do I find myself worrying about the process and the outcome?

You have promised you will never leave me and that with you, all things are possible. I have no reason to be anxious about my future. My path, when fully surrendered to you, is determined by your purpose and in your wisdom. As I walk through this life following your lead, I have confidence that each step I take will be planted in the footprint you have placed in front of me.

From this day forward, my own hands do not govern my life. I'm totally the Lord's, and I desire his complete control over all I do. I believe that he will accomplish all the works he created for me. Through them, he will be glorified.

God of All Hope

I hope in You, O Lord;
You will answer, O Lord my God.

PSALM 38:15 NASB

Father, ever since the day I gave my heart to you, I have placed all my confidence in you. I know that your Word says my hope will never be cut off, so I believe and wait in positive expectation of all you will accomplish in me. I know that all I need to do is come before your throne for you to attentively listen to my requests. I am certain that when I ask with the right motives and in the name of my Savior, you will answer.

If I abide in you, Scripture says that I will receive what I desire from you. I also know that you will overrule my desires when it's in my best interest and give me what is right in your incomparable will. I praise you for hearing me and caring so deeply about my needs. I wait in anticipation of your response that is birthed out of your goodness and perfect love for me.

There is nowhere else to go but to the Father; everything that I need comes from his gracious hand. I commit to depending on him all my days, for he alone leads me to abundant life.

Good and Faithful Servant

God has given each of you a gift from his great variety of spiritual gifts. Use them well to serve one another.

1 PETER 4:10 NLT

Lord, I have often heard it said that you do not call the equipped; you equip those you have called. I wonder what my gift is. I know I have one, possibly more, but sometimes they seem all over the map and not fully developed.

I think I am missing something. Will you please show me what you have prepared for me and give me the confidence to step into my purpose? I know that I can do nothing without you, but I also believe your Word that says through Christ, I can do all things. The sky is not even the limit! I want to fulfill what you have placed me on this earth to do. I pray for the wisdom, insight, and courage to serve you well. Someday, I hope with my whole heart to hear: "Well done, good and faithful servant."

Before I was even conceived, the Creator had prepared works for me to do in advance. I declare that he will perform and complete everything he has placed me on earth to do for his glory.

Point to Him

Humble yourselves before the Lord,
and he will lift you up.

JAMES 4:10 NIV

Lord, after reading this verse today, I must confess that I have been trying to elevate myself. It isn't even from a desire to be noticed; it's the result of my poor self-esteem that fears I have nothing to offer. I have not been seeing myself through your eyes, so I have tried to create a fake appearance of perceived worth.

I want to put aside my pride and false humility and just seek you. I pray that people won't even see me and instead witness only you by experiencing the fragrance of Christ when I am present. All that really matters is that I make you known. I will trust you to position me in a way that takes attention off me and leads others to you.

My heavenly Father is the great and famous one. No one can ever compare to him. In his wisdom and generosity, he allows me to be part of his purposes. I will never seek applause for myself. I will always point to my all-powerful, miraculous God.

Living Word

The Word of God is alive and active. Sharper than any double-edged sword, it penetrates even to dividing soul and spirit, joints and marrow; it judges the thoughts and attitudes of the heart.

HEBREWS 4:12 NIV

Father, I must admit there are times I go on autopilot when I am reading my Bible. It happens when I dive in without asking your Holy Spirit to reveal truth to me. When I am reading a passage I have reviewed many times before, I tend to give into mental distractions. Then, I hear your voice. You call me to come to you and learn great and magnificent things I do not know.

You want me to be a student of the Word. Please help me be attentive and give me insight to understand the Scriptures. There is no other book that is alive like yours. Words can jump off the page and infuse themselves into my very being. Please allow your Word to penetrate my heart, take root in my mind, and make me more like your Son.

I declare that God's Word is living. It breathes life into my very soul as it convicts me and speaks his truth to me. I will open myself to the surgery of the Scripture to reveal and correct the motives of my heart.

Suffering for Christ

Rejoice inasmuch as you participate in the sufferings of Christ, so that you may be overjoyed when his glory is revealed.

1 PETER 4:13 NIV

Father, I have found myself the recipient of judgmental remarks and rejection because of my faith in you. Some of those comments have been directly delivered; others have surfaced in gossip. I know that Scripture says the world will hate me because of my commitment to you. I am okay with the general population being against me, but when it proceeds from the mouths of friends, it cuts deep.

The deeper I go with you, the more distance develops between myself and those I care for but who do not agree with me. Let my heart be at peace with that sad truth. I know I am right to align myself with you. Whatever I suffer on this earth is worth it if it ultimately brings you glory.

I am all in as a follower of Jesus. I am his child, his sheep, and his mouthpiece to all who are willing to listen. I will suffer to make his name known. Anything that attacks me because of the gospel is worth enduring, for I know Jesus is the truth. He has set me free.

Anything Is Possible

I can do everything through Christ,
who gives me strength.

PHILIPPIANS 4:13 NLT

Father, I know that the source of your abiding power for me is in your Son. In the moment, I often fail to recall that all things are possible through Jesus and that this capability is always at my disposal. This results in trying to accomplish the task in my own strength. How ridiculously shortsighted of me! It is my own mindless negligence that moves me to act abruptly and then suffer the consequences.

Ephesians 1:19-20 says that the power of those who believe is the same power you exerted when you raised Christ from the dead. Thank you for this tremendous, inexhaustible endowment you have given me. Please give me faith to always move forward in the miraculous, limitless, and fully available power of my Savior.

There is nothing I can't achieve, for God has given me everything I need in Christ to conquer anything in his name. As I go forward in his strength, no weapon forged against me can stand. I affirm that anything is possible, and nothing can be thwarted when it is done in the powerful name of Jesus Christ.

Living Water

"Whoever drinks of the water that I shall give him will never thirst. But the water that I shall give him will become in him a fountain of water springing up into everlasting life."

JOHN 4:14 NKJV

Lord, this verse brings me back to the Old Testament. Psalm 42 says, "As the deer pants for the water, so my soul pants for you, oh God. My soul thirsts for God, the living God. Where can I go and meet with God?" I am thankful that desire and question was answered in you, Jesus, when you revealed yourself as the living water.

You are the only one who can quench my longing and the longing of all humanity. You alone are the only source of salvation. You offer absolution and eternal life. I am so amazed at the lack of effort this provision required of me and the enormous sacrifice it demanded of you. I receive this enduring refreshment in humble gratitude; I offer my life in return for yours that was given for me.

I will never thirst again, for Jesus has filled me with living water that springs into eternal life. There is no other way but through him and no adequate solution for sin but his salvation. I will continue to drink from his fountain of life now and through eternity.

Our High Priest

We do not have a high priest who is unable to sympathize with our weaknesses, but one who in every respect has been tempted as we are, yet without sin.

HEBREWS 4:15 ESV

Savior, I am thankful that you don't just know my struggle with sin; you have personal experience. As you walked this earth, the Son of God in human flesh, you encountered every temptation that I will ever face, yet you withstood them and didn't yield to disobedience. You knew that in my own strength I would not have that same success, so you provided the way out.

I praise you, my high priest, for ripping the curtain open permanently by satisfying the necessary judgment for my sin at Calvary. Jesus, your grace has saved me from eternal separation from God. You paid my debt on the cross. When you said, "It is finished," it was my beginning. Through you my eternity was secured.

I declare that my high priest, Jesus Christ, is my Savior, the one who knows me and understands my frailties. He experienced the lure of sinful pleasure, but he rebuked and refused it. I will resist it too, for I am filled with the power of Christ to defy and conquer evil.

September

"Keep watch and pray,
so that you will not
give in to temptation.
For the spirit is willing,
but the body is weak!"

MATTHEW 26:41 NLT

Inwardly Renewed

Therefore we do not lose heart.
Though outwardly we are wasting away,
yet inwardly we are being renewed day by day.

2 Corinthians 4:16 niv

Great God, thank you for your grace and strength that infuses my innermost self. I come alive in your love, and my fear is turned to faith. No matter what I walk through, I know that you are with me. No matter how my body declines, you are renewing me on the inside. My soul and spirit will be strong in faith because your Spirit is alive in me.

I won't ignore the implications of my body, but I will not let the joy of my soul be dependent on the health of my body. I am being renewed, and I will continue to be renewed by you. Minister your strength, support, and wisdom and transform me from the inside out.

I declare that no matter what, I will face the day with courage. The Spirit of God is alive within me, and he is the source of all I need. He will revive and refresh my soul.

Full of Love

He makes the whole body fit together perfectly.
As each part does its own special work, it helps the
other parts grow, so that the whole body is healthy
and growing and full of love.

EPHESIANS 4:16 NLT

Jesus Christ, you are the head of your church, and I am a part of the body of believers. I know that I was not created to stand on my own. I am part of a larger whole, and you are the leader. Instead of trying to do what I was never meant to do, help me focus on my part. As I work in my gifts and do what you call me to do, I know that you will use me for your glory.

When I see another part of the body struggling, show me ways to support them. Thank you for your larger perspective and for being the leader that we all need. I don't have to control or manipulate others; that was never my job. I will look for ways to serve while also confidently doing what is mine to do. I trust others to be submitted to you as they do their part as well. May I be filled with your love today for you and for my brothers and sisters.

I declare that I will do my part to promote unity in the body of believers. I won't overstep and I will not shrink back. I will be fully me and trust the Lord with the rest.

Come Boldly

Let us come boldly to the throne of our gracious God. There we will receive his mercy, and we will find grace to help us when we need it most.

HEBREWS 4:16 NLT

Gracious God, I come boldly to your throne today. I enter into your presence to receive your mercy. You have what I am longing for. You have the grace I am so desperate for. You have the strength I require. You have the determination and the confidence I need.

Fill me with the perfect peace of your presence and lift the heavy burdens off my shoulders as you fill me with your life-giving light. Teach me with your wisdom. Give me your perspective for my limited understanding. I want to know you more. I won't stay away; in the fullness of your presence, I press in to know you more. Thank you for the open invitation.

I declare that there is nothing that can keep me from the love of God. I will come boldly before him and trust him to meet me with mercy and grace.

God Is Love

We have come to know and have believed the love which God has for us. God is love, and the one who abides in love abides in God, and God abides in him. By this, love is perfected with us, so that we may have confidence in the day of judgment; because as He is, so also are we in this world.

1 John 4:16-17 NASB

Compassionate Father, you are pure, living love. There is nothing that you do without mercy. There are no decisions you make outside of the kindness of your heart. You are love, and any expression of love I live out in this life is a glimpse of you. I want to abide in your love. I want to be so surrounded, so filled, and so encapsulated by your love that it naturally flows out of what I do, how I speak, and how I relate to others.

Your love does not discriminate. It does not self-protect, and it does not seek its own gain. It is ever-expansive and reaches beyond itself. Help me to choose compassion over judgment. Transform me in your image, and may I be a living reflection of your wonderful mercy and kindness.

God is love, and in him there is no shadow of evil. He is better than I can imagine. I can't exaggerate his kindness. I will live large in love today, and I will not let fear keep me stuck in small-minded behavior.

Lasting Glory

Our present troubles are small and won't last very long.
Yet they produce for us a glory that vastly outweighs
them and will last forever! So we don't look at the
troubles we can see now; rather, we fix our gaze on
things that cannot be seen.

2 Corinthians 4:17-18 nlt

Great God, thank you for the promised goodness in the
fullness of your kingdom come. Even though I can't escape
the troubles of this life, I don't want to get so caught up in
them that I forget you are with me. I don't want to be so
burdened by temporary pain that I fail to see that every
day has an end and every season a limited cycle.

I am grateful for the promise of a new dawn and new
seasons approaching. Even so, may I not fail to recognize
where your mercy meets me in my mess. Show me what
you are doing even now in my heartbreak. I trust you.

*Nothing on this earth will last forever—no pain, no trial,
and no trouble. There is more to look forward to than what
I leave behind. I declare that I will look ahead with hope
today, for God is good, and he is faithful.*

Perfect Love

Such love has no fear, because perfect love expels all fear. If we are afraid, it is for fear of punishment, and this shows that we have not fully experienced his perfect love.

1 JOHN 4:18 NLT

In you, Perfect One, there is no fear. You are not a power-hungry leader who rules with threats. You are not a cold-hearted ruler who punishes to make an example. Everything you do is done in love even when it feels painful. I recognize that not everything I experience in this life can be understood or wrapped up neat with a bow.

Still, I know your character. I know what you are like. You are full of merciful kindness and always reach out in love. Your grace saves me from my propensity toward sin and retaliation. Your redemption makes all things new in you, and I am made new in you. I will not live with fear's rigid requirements keeping me small. I will live in the largeness of your love.

Fear limits me; love propels me into freedom. I choose to live with love as my motivation. I will look for ways to expand in compassion today, and I will not let fear keep me from taking risks in love.

Every Need Met

My God will meet all your needs according to the riches
of his glory in Christ Jesus.

PHILIPPIANS 4:19 NIV

Christ Jesus, you are the supplier of all I require. Meet
me now in my need and fill me with the goodness and
abundance of your living love. You see what I need today.
Where hopelessness has set in, breathe in fresh vision.
Where disappointment has broken me down, minister
healing, comfort, and strength. Where troubles have
wrapped fear around my heart, loosen its grip with your
perfect love.

For all I am dealing with and all I thought I knew, expand
my understanding of your great love through deeper
fellowship with your Spirit today.

*I declare that I trust the Lord to meet the needs I can't on my
own. I know he will not just do it; he will give me more than
enough grace, mercy, and love to keep persevering in his
presence. I am submitted to his love's leadership in my life.*

Sun of Righteousness

For you who fear my name,
the sun of righteousness shall rise
with healing in its wings.

MALACHI 4:2 ESV

Righteous Lord, I look to you like a flower looks to the sun. I depend on your rains the way the earth does. I need you more than I can say. Rise, as the Scriptures say, with healing in your wings. Rise upon me now. Shine on me, and I will soak up your life-giving light. Rain down on me, and I will revive in your presence. Feed me with the sustenance of your Spirit. Refresh me in your waters.

You see the areas of my life that await your healing touch. You see the rubble and the ashes, and I long for your restoration power to move. Come, Lord. Reveal yourself. Rise upon me, and bring your healing to my soul, spirit, body, and mind.

I declare that as I look to the Son, he will shine his light on my life. He will revive my hope and refresh my courage. He is all I need.

He Is Greater

You, dear children, are from God and have overcome
them, because the one who is in you is greater than the
one who is in the world.

1 JOHN 4:4 NIV

Great God, I am your child. I am yours! Thank you for the
promise of greater things to come; they will be greater
than anything I've ever known. Your kingdom will come,
and your will shall be done on earth as it is in heaven. The
greater glory of your kingdom will come through. You will
rule and reign in complete authority, and every knee will
bow before you. Every tongue will confess that you, Jesus
Christ, are Lord.

Until that day, strengthen me from the inside out with
your empowering grace. I know that you are greater than
anything I face, and I trust you. I will overcome, for you
have already overcome every foe.

*I declare that God's Spirit within me is greater than any
fear, shame, trial, or corruptive force I face. I will trust his
resurrection power, and I will walk boldly with the promise
of his help in every circumstance.*

Comforting Words

Your words have comforted those who fell,
and you have strengthened those who could not stand.

JOB 4:4 NCV

Comforter, thank you for your promised help. Thank you for being near. Please go beyond my desperate belief in your presence and help me experience your wrap-around love in my life. I long for a fresh touch of your grace.

Comfort me in my grief and draw near to me in my sorrow. Lift my eyes to see that you are already closer than I knew. Speak your living words over my broken heart. Bring relief to my dry and weary soul with the refreshing waters of your Spirit. Strengthen me, encourage me, and heal me. I am yours, and I rely on you.

I am not alone in my pain. The Spirit of God is my greatest comfort and strength. I will look for ways to comfort others when I am able, and I will rely on the help of the Spirit and his people to encourage me when I can't stand on my own.

Pray about Everything

Don't worry about anything; instead, pray about everything. Tell God what you need, and thank him for all he has done. Then you will experience God's peace, which exceeds anything we can understand. His peace will guard your hearts and minds as you live in Christ Jesus.

PHILIPPIANS 4:6-7 NLT

God, instead of giving into worry and anxiety about unknowns, I will offer them to you today in prayer. May prayer become as consistent as breathing to me. Thank you for all you have already done! I won't forget the ways you have faithfully come through for me and those who have called on your name.

I will not hold myself back from laying everything out before you today. I want to communicate openly and freely with you until my whole day is filled with prayer. Guard my heart and mind with your perfect peace. I trust you, so why should I worry?

As I pray about everything, God's peace will surround, fill, and sustain me. Nothing is too insignificant to share with him. He cares about it all. I will give him access to every piece of my heart, my mind, and my life.

Continue in Love

Dear friends, let us continue to love one another,
for love comes from God. Anyone who loves is a
child of God and knows God.

1 JOHN 4:7 NLT

Loving Father, thank you for the reminder that love is
always worth it. It is a beautiful pursuit to look for ways to
love others the way that you love me. I don't want to fool
myself into thinking I am like you when my actions, words,
and motivations are not from a place of love. Your kindness
doesn't need my approval. You are infinitely merciful; where
you do not put conditions on your love, I will not either.

Help me, Lord, to live as a reflection of your pure
compassion. You constantly surprise and encourage me in
your love. May I do the same for others.

*I declare that when I choose to live with larger love, I live as
a reflection of Christ. Perfect love does not come from fear.
I trust that God knows what he's doing and what he's called
me to do. I will follow his path of laid-down love.*

God's Heir

You are no longer a slave, but God's child;
and since you are his child,
God has made you also an heir.

GALATIANS 4:7 NIV

Lord, as your child, I am also an heir to your kingdom. What a wonderful and humbling reality that is! Everything you possess is available to me through your Son. You don't withhold any goodness from those who bear your name. Until we are living in the fullness of your kingdom, I will trust you. I will press in to know you more and more. I will grow up in your love, grace, and mercy. I will bear the fruit of your Spirit as I remain submitted to your ways.

I am your child and your heir. What a wonderful gift, and what a wonderful reality. Thank you, Father.

I declare that I am a child of the living God, and I am his heir. Everything he offers to his kingdom is accessible to me. I will use these wondrous resources to bring him glory and witness about his saving grace.

Submit

Submit yourselves, then, to God.
Resist the devil, and he will flee from you.

JAMES 4:7 NIV

Good Father, I am submitted to you, and my life is in your hands. I withhold nothing. You can have my fears, my shame, and every cycle of sin that has kept me stuck. I want you more than I want my own way. I want your freedom more than I want the empty promises of this world.

Let your love uncover every area that has been hidden. Let it saturate every dry and cracked place within my heart and life. I will not follow the foolishness of self-protection or shame-based thinking. I know that as I submit myself to you and resist every other power, I will stand strong in your love.

Nothing is worth my loss of freedom in Christ's love. He has set me free, so I am truly free. I will resist the pull of quick fixes and press into the Lord for healing and abundance.

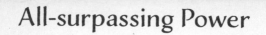
All-surpassing Power

We have this treasure in jars of clay to show that this all-surpassing power is from God and not from us. We are hard pressed on every side, but not crushed; perplexed, but not in despair; persecuted, but not abandoned; struck down, but not destroyed.

2 CORINTHIANS 4:7-9 NIV

Mighty God, though I am hard-pressed, I am not crushed. Though I am perplexed, I will not despair. Though I may face persecution, I am never abandoned. I may be struck down, but I will not be destroyed. Your power is greater than anything the world can throw at me. Your living love is more reliable than the sunrise, and it is more consistent than the waves on the shore.

I trust you to help, guide, and strengthen me every step of this life. You are my holy hope, and though there will be loss, brokenness, and pain in this life, there is also an abundance of mercy, blessings, and goodness in your presence. Move in mighty ways, Lord, for I depend on you.

I declare that God's power is able to do more than I can imagine. I rely on his power to move mightily in my life and not on my own strength. I am holding on to hope; I am holding on to him.

Draw Near

Draw near to God,
and he will draw near to you.

JAMES 4:8 ESV

God, I draw near to you today. Please draw even closer to me as I do. Wrap around me with the tangible presence of your Spirit. Fill me with courage, hope, and relief. Flood my senses with your goodness. Relieve the pain I can't seem to escape. Minister comfort and revive my hope.

I come to you with all I have: every joy, every expectation, every longing, and every question. All of it. There's no reason to keep any of it to myself. I know that you won't ever turn me away. Speak your wise words of life over my circumstances and give me your perspective. Be near, Lord.

I declare that when I turn to God, I find he is already turned toward me. As I draw near to him, he draws near to me. He is so much closer than I realize.

Dwell in Peace

In peace I will lie down and sleep,
for you alone, LORD, make me dwell in safety.

PSALM 4:8 NIV

Prince of Peace, set me securely in the safety of your hand.
Do not let fear keep me from resting in your love. You said
that your perfect love casts out all fear. Will you fill me up
with your kindness? My worries dim and lose their power
over my mind when I am awash in your compassion.

I don't want toxic thinking to keep me from trusting you. I
don't want to war against my own thoughts. Show me how
to offer compassion to myself just as you offer compassion.
Teach me to observe my thoughts and to not embody the
unneeded ones. May I learn to dwell in your peace in every
moment even as I let go of the need to control. I love you,
and I trust you.

*As I release the compulsion to go over situations in my
mind over and over again, I find the peace of God replaces
it. I will sleep soundly, and I will rest in his safe love. He is
bigger than my mistakes, and he will never fail.*

Good Shepherd

He tends his flock like a shepherd: He gathers the lambs in his arms and carries them close to his heart; he gently leads those that have young.

ISAIAH 40:11 NIV

Lord, you are the shepherd of my soul. You lead me, you care for me, and you protect me. You will not let me be lost to the wolves. You will not let me wander outside of your care. Thank you for your patience with me. Thank you for your tenderness. You love me so well; you love me more than anyone else can.

I will trust you, follow you, and depend on you all the days of my life. Even when it seems as if you have left me, I know you are pursuing me still. You will not let evil overcome me. You always keep a watchful eye, and I can rest in your tender care.

I declare that God is my Good Shepherd. He will not let me go, and he will not lead me to destruction. He is better than any other, and I trust him.

Infinite Understanding

How can you say the LORD does not see your troubles?
The LORD is the everlasting God, the Creator of all the
earth. He never grows weak or weary. No one can
measure the depths of his understanding.

ISAIAH 40:27-28 NLT

Creator, thank you for seeing my troubles. Thank you
for knowing what's on my mind before I can say a word.
Thank you for seeing what is coming before it is here. I
trust you to guide me; I trust you to keep me. I trust you
in everything. I look to you for wisdom, and I lean on your
strength.

I'm so grateful that you never grow weak or weary. You
never get distracted, and you can't be fooled. What an
encouragement to my heart! Care for me like a mother
cares for her child. Tend to my wounds and heal me with
the oil of your presence. I rely on your care.

*I declare that as I lean on the Lord, I can trust him with
everything I can and can't see. I will not worry about
whether God can handle my problems. I choose to rest in
his loving care and trust him to do what I can't.*

More Available

He gives strength to those who are tired
and more power to those who are weak.

ISAIAH 40:29 NCV

Powerful One, I am so grateful for this moment. It is a fresh opportunity to receive your mercy. The portion of your grace is always plentiful and always more than enough for me. Where I am tired, revive me in your strength. Where I am weak, offer me the power of your presence.

I am so limited, Lord. I am limited in love, in understanding, and in every capacity I can think of. You, however, are limitless. You are abundant in grace, mercy, power, joy, peace, hope, love, and all good things. Through your Spirit, you always have more to offer me than I could ever dream of. I yield to you, Lord. I look to you for all I need right now and in every moment. Fill me with the generosity of your kingdom.

I declare that as I follow the Lord, he will renew me in his strength. He will never leave me to fend for myself. He is my source of strength, power, and all blessings. He is my sustenance.

Renewed and Refreshed

Those who wait for the LORD shall renew their strength,
they shall mount up with wings like eagles,
they shall run and not be weary,
they shall walk and not faint.

ISAIAH 40:31 NRSV

Lord, I wait on you today. I invite your presence to come alive within me right now. I know that you hear my prayers, and I know that you answer. Come close, Lord. Reveal what is on your heart today. Give me greater perspective of your love and fill my heart with courage in your mercy.

As I wait on you, will you renew my strength? You give me grace that empowers me to persevere. You give me rest when I can't keep going. You carry me when my legs give way. You refresh and renew my spirit within me. Please do it again, Lord.

As I wait on the Lord today, I am met with the generosity of his love. He will fill me with all I need to get through each moment with grace and kindness. He is my abundant source.

His Word Lasts

The grass withers, the flower fades,
but the word of our God stands forever.

ISAIAH 40:8 NASB

Unchanging One, thank you for the faithfulness of your character and your promises. You do not wither or change. You do not fade or fluctuate. You are always constant; you are always true. You are always a man of your word. You simply are.

Living in a world full of transition and change, my heart sometimes needs these reminders. I know people of integrity, but no one is as consistent as you. I trust that you will continue to work out your promises in this world. I trust that you will continue to move in power in my life. Your Word remains, and it is living and active. Complete your will in me, Lord. I am yours.

I declare that the Word holds our Lord's promises. His nature is faithfulness. He will never change, and he will not fail. I will continue to see his goodness in the land of the living.

Consider This

Happy are those who consider the poor;
the LORD delivers them in the day of trouble.

PSALM 41:1 NRSV

Lord, I can't escape your compassion, and I can't hide from your mercy. May I not get so distracted by other things in life that I forget to care for the poor and lend a voice to the vulnerable. May I never be so caught up in my own story that I stop listening to the stories of others.

In your kingdom, we are all brothers and sisters. No one is without mercy, without value, or without your help. May I live with your honor as my own and reach out in generosity whenever possible. I want to lift and encourage those who need it. Help me to keep first things first in my life as it is in your kingdom.

God cares for the poor and vulnerable and so will I. I declare that God's compassion is my source of mercy, and there is a never-ending supply. I will not turn a blind eye to the disheartened and discouraged. I will look for ways to encourage them and lighten their load.

A Strong Help

Don't be afraid, for I am with you.
Don't be discouraged, for I am your God.
I will strengthen you and help you.
I will hold you up with my victorious right hand.

ISAIAH 41:10 NLT

God, I need you. Repeatedly in the Bible, I see your encouragement to not worry. I don't want fear to sideline me in my own life. Fill me with the strength of your Spirit and give me courage to press on while knowing you are with me.

You do not say, "Don't be afraid...don't be discouraged" to people who are full of confidence and hope. You say it to the weary and the wavering. Thank you for that reminder. I am weary, Lord. I am wavering. Be my strength and my help. Uphold me with your victorious right hand.

Even though I feel weary and fearful, I will not let that stop me from turning to the Lord. I will build up my confidence in him by looking to his faithfulness. His track record is incomparable. He is so good! He will help me.

Integrity Matters

Because of my integrity you uphold me
and set me in your presence forever.

PSALM 41:12 NIV

Lord, thank you for your Spirit who constantly works to enlarge my capacity for love. As I follow you and commit to your kingdom ways, I am compelled to live honestly and rightly. May integrity guard my heart. May honor for you and for others keep me from going astray.

I know that how I choose to live my life matters, and I won't pretend that it doesn't. Your love has liberated me to choose your ways. They are so much better than the ways of this world. Your path of love will never steer me wrong, so I'm dedicated to keep following you on it. Help me, encourage me, and strengthen me along the way.

I have been redeemed by love, and love's liberty is mine. I choose to walk in integrity according to God's will and ways. I will continue to follow him and his wisdom today.

No Stopping God

"I know that you can do anything,
and no one can stop you."

JOB 42:2 NLT

What you start, God, you finish. What you vow to do, you follow through on in faithfulness. I trust that even when I can't see how you are working things out, you are doing it, and you are doing it well. I know that you can do anything, so I won't hold back even my wildest requests from you. I know that you will do what is right, even if it would not be my preference.

You take so much more into account than my preferences. You are just and true, and you are full of mercy in all you do. I can't manipulate you, and I don't want to. I lay my heart out before you, and I trust you to do infinitely better things than I could imagine.

God can do anything, and no one can stop him. He is better than all humanity. He is more faithful than anyone. He is full of good intentions toward all he has made. I will trust him to faithfully fulfill his Word and weave his mercy through my life.

Night Songs

By day the LORD directs his love,
at night his song is with me—
a prayer to the God of my life.

PSALM 42:8 NIV

Lord, thank you for directing your love toward me. It is not vain of me to say this; it is who you are. I am completely and wholly loved by you. Sing your songs of peace, deliverance, and hope over me as I sleep at night. Encourage me with the fellowship of your Spirit by day.

My life is a prayer to you; my heart is an offering. My song is a loving response to your goodness. Fill my heart with more of you and calm my worries with the joy of your presence. There is nothing better than your nearness, and there is no sweeter joy than your companionship.

The Lord of all sings over me, and I will offer him the song of my heart. He keeps me in perfect peace, for my mind is turned to him. He has my attention, and he has my affection.

Redeemed and Chosen

"Fear not, for I have redeemed you;
I have called you by name, you are mine."

ISAIAH 43:1 ESV

Redeemer, thank you for calling me your own. You called my name before I could recognize your voice. You thought of me before I was even formed in my mother's womb. What a wonderful creator, father, and friend! I come alive in the delight of your love.

I belong to you. I am yours, and you are mine. I will not let fear keep me from moving forward in you. I will not let it keep me from taking the risk to love you and others without condition. You are my source and supply, and your waters are always fresh and flowing. Where my understanding has stalled and my heart has become stale, revive me in the flowing fountains of your revelation.

I declare that I am loved, I am redeemed, and I am chosen. I belong to God the Father, Jesus Christ the Son, and the Holy Spirit. I am fully accepted by the Triune God, and I am found in him. Hallelujah!

Rivers of Blessing

"I am about to do something new.
See, I have already begun! Do you not see it?
I will make a pathway through the wilderness.
I will create rivers in the dry wasteland."

ISAIAH 43:19 NLT

Restorer, you are always doing something new in your mercy. You are not prescriptive, and what you do is never without thought. You meet us with the overwhelming goodness of your presence right where we are and exactly how we need it.

I trust that you are not finished with me yet. I trust that I have not tasted your goodness for the last time and that I have not seen the pinnacle of your love in my life. Make a pathway where there is none and create rivers in the dry wastelands where I tread. Make gardens of your glory grow in the desolate places of my life. You are a restorer; you are the Redeemer. I look to you for renewed hope and fresh vision.

The glorious Lord of all creation is still working in my life. He is still meeting me with mercy. He is still faithful. He is still good. I cling to that truth today and encourage my soul in his faithfulness.

Trust Him

"When you pass through the waters, I will be with you;
and when you pass through the rivers,
they will not sweep over you.
When you walk through the fire, you will not be burned;
the flames will not set you ablaze."

ISAIAH 43:2 NIV

Faithful One, though the storms of life come, I trust that you will never let me go. You will be with me in raging rivers and overflowing waters of trouble. You will not let the trials of this life sweep me away. I remain rooted and grounded in your love. Even when I walk through the fires of testing, I will not be burned. You keep me safe.

Lord, you are my encouragement and my strength. Thank you for your promised faithfulness. I trust you more than any other. I trust you to do what you said you would. I trust that you will never abandon me no matter how hard life gets. Thank you for your consistent presence.

I declare that my heart trusts the Lord's faithfulness and goodness more than the harsh realities of this life. He will continue to do what he started, and he will make a way where I can see none. He is the anchor of my soul, and my hope is in him.

October

Answer me when I pray to you,
my God who does what is right.
Make things easier for me
when I am in trouble.
Have mercy on me and
hear my prayer.

PSALM 4:1 NCV

Redemption Power

"I have swept away offences like a cloud,
your sins like the morning mist.
Return to me, for I have redeemed you."

ISAIAH 44:22 NIV

Savior, thank you for taking my shame and separating me from it. You have forgiven me and purified me; you have removed my offences. Like a morning mist, they evaporated in your presence. I will return to you, and continue to return to you, all the days of my life. You are my redemption and my saving grace. Why would I wander and struggle on my own when you have called me and welcomed me into your kingdom with open arms?

I want to live in the freedom of your love, in the endless delight of your affection, and in the power of your purposes. Thank you, Lord, for not holding my past against me. As far as the east is from the west, that is how far you have removed my transgressions. Thank you!

I have been redeemed by love, and it is in the freedom of that love that I now live. I will not hold against myself what God does not. I will not hold against others what God has wiped away. I am free in his mercy.

Secret Riches

"I will give you hidden treasures,
riches stored in secret places,
so that you may know that I am the Lord,
the God of Israel, who summons you by name."

ISAIAH 45:3 NIV

Lord, there is no greater treasure in the heavens or on the earth than knowing you. This is not some far-off ideal that can't be attained. You have drawn me to yourself in loving kindness, and I come to you through Jesus Christ. It is a beautiful gift to be known by you and to spend my life getting to know you in return. I long for the hidden treasures stored in the secret places of your presence.

You are the one who called me at first and who calls me still. You call my name, and I come running. Here I am, Lord. Reveal your heart to me in greater ways today.

There is wealth in the wisdom of God, and there is bounty in knowing him. I give myself to this holy pursuit. I want to know him more than I want success in this life. As I pursue him, he reveals more of himself, more of his wisdom, and more of his kingdom. What a delightful dance this is!

Eternal Refuge

God is our refuge and strength,
an ever-present help in trouble.

PSALM 46:1 NIV

God, you are my refuge and my strength. You are an ever-present help in trouble. You are constant in my life; you never let me go. I depend on you, and I lean on your understanding over my own. I press in to know you more, especially when the pressures of life press in on me. I run into the safe place of your presence. You are always available, and you never turn me away. Thank you!

I don't want to ever take your love for granted, but we both know I will at times. I am so grateful that you do not require perfection from me. You just ask for a willing and humble heart. I love you, Lord. I submit to you. I run to you. Thank you for always waiting with open arms. I am humbled by your extravagant mercy.

I declare that the Lord is my strength and my shelter. He is my help in every trial and trouble. He is my constant source of blessings and my rock of refuge in every season of the soul. He is my safe place.

Be Still and Know

"Be still, and know that I am God.
I will be exalted among the nations,
I will be exalted in the earth!"

PSALM 46:10 ESV

Great God, I quiet myself before you now. I take deep, cleansing breaths to calm my nervous system as I focus my attention on you. I sit still, breathing in your presence and directing my heart to the present moment. This is where you meet me. This moment is all I have, and you are near. You are here in your fullness and love. You, who can never be diminished, have come to meet with me. You are with me now, and I am grateful.

As I commune with your Spirit, may your wisdom speak to me. As deep calls to deep, so your still, small voice speaks to the depths of my soul. I trust you, Lord. I am yours.

I declare that whenever I am overwhelmed, I will take a few moments to close my eyes and be still before the Lord. I will direct my attention to his faithfulness and my mind to his goodness.

Forever and Ever

This God is our God for ever and ever;
he will be our guide even to the end.

PSALM 48:14 NIV

Eternal One, I will follow you to the end. There is no one better, no one wiser, and no one more merciful than you are. I give you my life; lead me on. You are my God, and you are the God of the ages. My life is but a short breath in the scope of eternity, yet you think of me. Thank you for calling me, choosing me, and loving me so completely.

I am caught up in the crux of creation's longing to know you. I am but a microcosm of creation, yet my longing joins with others who are being united with you. I am from you, and I will return to you. In the meantime, lead me through the peaks and valleys of this life.

I declare that I trust the Lord and the Bible. I trust that from age to age, he remains the same. He is loyal in love, considerate in kindness, and powerful in redemption. I will follow him to the end.

Never Forgotten

"How could a loving mother forget her nursing child and
not deeply love the one she bore?
Even if a there is a mother who forgets her child,
I could never, no never, forget you."

ISAIAH 49:15 TPT

Loving God, thank you for caring for me so tenderly. When
I consider a mother's ferocious and tender love for her
child, I can't help but be moved by the truth that you love
me even more passionately. You said that you would never
forget your people. You do not rescind your promises
because you are always faithful. What you say is truth, and
I trust your love.

Lord, remind me how fully you know me and care for me.
Refresh my hope in the life-giving waters of your presence.
Revive my weary heart in your nearness. Hold me, Lord. I
just need to be held by you.

*The Lord's love is more ferocious than a mother bear, and
it is more constant than a mother's care. I am fully seen,
known, and loved. I am held by mercy's embrace today.*

Engraved

"See, I have engraved you on the palms of my hands;
your walls are ever before me."

ISAIAH 49:16 NIV

Jesus, thank you for your sacrifice. The lengths you went to show the Father's love are too much for me to fully comprehend. You gave your life for us and laid it down humbly and freely. You became fully human and lived among us. You experienced hunger, weariness, and the joy of fellowship. You experienced betrayal as well as adoration.

You lived the full human experience. You even endured death on a cross so that you could render the grave powerless three days later. The best part? You did it all for love. Thank you for the power of your resurrection and for the abundance of your mercy. I am yours, Lord.

My Lord Jesus sees what my life entails, and he knows my struggles. He does not turn a blind eye. He understands. I am free in his love, and I will live to know him more.

Restoration Is Coming

The God of all grace, who called you to his eternal glory in Christ, after you have suffered a little while, will himself restore you and make you strong, firm and steadfast.

1 PETER 5:10 NIV

Gracious God, thank you for the promise of restoration and redemption. I do not enjoy suffering loss, grief, and disappointment. Thankfully, you have said that it is not my end. Grief will not destroy me; despair will not be my portion. You are full of mercy right here and now. You promise to work all things out for my good and for your glory, and I trust that you will do that with every part of my story.

Do not leave me in my pain, Lord. Draw close and whisper your words of life. They are refreshment to my soul. I trust that you will restore me and make me strong, firm, and steadfast. Come quickly.

God is full of grace in every moment. He will empower me to persevere today with his gracious presence, and I trust that he will bring about restoration and redemption in his timing. I hold on to hope.

Blessed in All Things

"Blessed are those who are persecuted
for righteousness' sake,
For theirs is the kingdom of heaven."

MATTHEW 5:10 NKJV

Lord, I don't want to take your Word lightly. I don't want to fool myself into thinking that I can escape the inevitable suffering that comes with being human. No one escapes hardship. No one evades loss.

When I am confronted with the pains of humanity, will you encourage my heart in your eternal truth? I will keep on following after you no matter what. Your ways are better than my own. Your love is worth every sacrifice I could ever make. I love you more than I love my comfort. You are the way, the truth, and the life, and I follow you.

I declare that no matter what I face in this life—whatever hardship, loss, or persecution—I am more than a conqueror through Christ. He is my victory, and his kingdom is my home. He is my holy hope, and I won't give up on him, for he never gives up on me.

Shielded by Love

You bless the godly, O LORD;
you surround them with your shield of love.

PSALM 5:12 NIV

Protector, thank you for being my shield and strength. You are my support and my source. You are full of loving kindness in all you do, and I know you will never change. When I do not understand how you are working your mercy in my life, draw me close to your heart. Give me the perspective of your eternal viewpoint. Give me eyes to see and ears to hear what you are doing and what you are saying.

I want to be surrounded by you all the days of my life. I want to live in the light of your kingdom and move in the power of your grace. Fill me up with your love, surround me with your light, and break through the confining walls of fear with your perfect peace.

The Lord blesses those who look to him. I look to him today for all I need. He is my source of strength, hope, and joy. There is no one like him.

Utter Confidence

This is the confidence we have in approaching God: that if we ask anything according to his will, he hears us.

1 John 5:14 niv

Great God, I know that you welcome me with the open arms of a loving father. You are waiting for me to turn and return to you when I go off on my own way. There is no reason to fear how I will be received in your presence, for you are good, merciful, and true. You are full of righteousness, and you are my righteousness. I don't have to prove a thing to you. You know me through and through, and you love me as I am.

I run into your arms today without holding anything back. Meet me with your overwhelming love and answer the cries of my heart with your faithfulness. I long for you more than anything else today.

I declare that I can approach God with confidence because he has welcomed me. I have an open invitation into his presence; I will not spend another moment in hesitation.

Things to Think About

Keep your thoughts continually fixed on all that is authentic and real, honorable and admirable, beautiful and respectful, pure and holy, merciful and kind.

PHILIPPIANS 4:8 TPT

Lord, as I read this verse, my heart leapt a little. Your kingdom is better than the governments of this world. Your standard is higher and purer, and it is full of good fruit. I will meditate on your Word today to redirect my thoughts to that which is authentic and real.

I will turn my attention to the honorable and admirable around me. I will look for the beautiful and respectful in my relationships with others. I will think about what is pure and holy in your sight, and I will focus in on that which is merciful and kind. As I search for these things in the world around me, I know that I won't go wrong if I steer by your star. In them, there you are.

I declare that the goodness of God is present in the world in these fruits of his kingdom. I will look for them like I look for treasure. I will choose to direct my gaze to them, and I will rejoice when I find them.

Honor to Blessing

"Honor your father and your mother, as the Lord your God has commanded you, that your days may be long, and that it may be well with you in the land which the Lord your God is giving you."

DEUTERONOMY 5:16 NKJV

Lord God, thank you for the wisdom of your Word. Thank you for the insight you have given us so that we may live freely in your kingdom ways. I know that honor begets honor in your kingdom. Please teach me what honor truly means to you. I know that you do not require blind obedience; you want a living relationship.

This must also be what you want in our family systems. May I honor those closest to me by heeding their wisdom and taking their perspectives into account. May I show respect even when there is disagreement. May connections remain intact even through conflict, and may I move through them with grace, compassion, and honor.

I declare that I will honor those in my life with my consideration. I will act with kindness, love, and mercy. I will listen to those who know me well and take their wisdom into account in my decisions.

Powerful Prayers

Confess your sins to each other and pray for each other so that you may be healed. The prayer of a righteous person is powerful and effective.

JAMES 5:16 NIV

Healer, I want to become more and more like you in my prayer life as well as in my relationships. I want to reflect your kindness, truth, and power in all I do. Thank you for your example of a humility that does not consider the self as more important than any other.

I choose to humble myself before you and others today. Where there has been sin or selfishness in my life, I will confess it today and seek prayer for it. Your Word says that the prayer of a righteous person is powerful and effective. You are my righteousness, and it is in your authority that I live, move, and have my being. May your power be evident in my submitted life.

I declare that today is the day of my breakthrough. I will not hold back from doing my part in confession, prayer, and seeking reconciliation. I am able to do hard things because Christ is with me. He will lead me into my breakthrough!

New in Christ

If anyone is in Christ, he is a new creation.
The old has passed away; behold, the new has come.

2 CORINTHIANS 5:17 ESV

Christ Jesus, thank you for the renewal I have found in you. Living in relationship with you, I am made new. My old ways of doing things do not define my future. I rely on you to transform me continually as I pursue wholeness and healing. I recognize that I have agency in my own development, and I will not neglect my part.

Thank you for the redemption you have sown, and are still sowing, into my story. There is nothing too far gone that you can't restore. There is no hope too lofty that you can't fulfill. With you, the impossible becomes possible. I know it's true because I've already experienced your resurrection power in my heart.

I am in Christ; therefore, I am new in him. Today I am fully accepted, fully loved, and fully alive in him. He is restoring me and redeeming what was lost. He is making all things new, and he will continue to do so.

Higher View

We have stopped evaluating others from a human point of view. At one time we thought of Christ merely from a human point of view. How differently we know him now!

2 Corinthians 5:16 nlt

Great God, how grateful I am that there is a difference between your viewpoint and my own. As I fellowship with you through your Spirit, you reveal a better perspective and transform my thoughts from what I once knew. Give me the eyes of your compassion when I am looking at others. May I see them through the lens of your mercy and the power of their identity in you. You are their Maker as much as you are mine.

Renew my mind in the expansive wisdom of your kingdom and give me greater clarity to call out the imprints of your goodness in every person. I want to know you more, to be transformed by your love, and to walk in the freedom of its power. Thank you.

I declare that God's views are better than my own, so I won't rely on my own understanding. I press in to know him more, to be like him, and to experience more of his compassionate heart through fellowship.

Ministry of Reconciliation

God has made all things new,
and reconciled us to himself,
and given us the ministry of reconciling others to God.

2 CORINTHIANS 5:18 TPT

Redeemer, thank you for your reconciliation. Thank you for doing all that had to be done in order for me to know you in Spirit and in truth. You made the way where there was none, and you continually lead me to the fullness of the Father. There is nothing better than your way.

Who else could break the chains of sin, shame, fear, and death and set us free in lavish love? It is you, Jesus, and I am so very thankful. I choose to follow you today and I look for ways to minister reconciliation to others. Where have I turned a cold shoulder, will you help me lean in with tenderness and compassion? Speak Lord; I am listening.

God has given me every kindness. Now, I get to partner with him in offering kindness to others. Instead of throwing up my personal defenses, I will look for ways to extend mercy.

Extravagant Love

Continue to walk surrendered to the extravagant love
of Christ, for he surrendered his life as a sacrifice for us.
His great love for us was pleasing to God, like an aroma
of adoration—a sweet healing fragrance.

EPHESIANS 5:2 TPT

Jesus, I continue to surrender my heart to you. Your
extravagant love is the source of my strength, joy, and hope.
You refresh and renew me in your presence. You fill me up
when I am empty. You are all I need, and I need you so!

May your love fuel my own until my life becomes an aroma
of adoration before the Father. I want to live as a sweet,
healing fragrance in a world where death and decay are
rampant. Your love is better than life itself. It is pure, it is
powerful, and it is more than anyone could describe. I want
to know you more. Fill me up from the inside out and let
my life overflow with the goodness of your kindness.

*I declare that my life, my heart, and my very being are
surrendered to the extravagant love of Christ. He is more
than enough for me and knowing him is indescribably
sweet. I am alive in his love.*

Incomparable Goodness

The Holy Spirit produces this kind of fruit in our lives: love, joy, peace, patience, kindness, goodness, faithfulness.

GALATIANS 5:22 NLT

Spirit, I want my life to reflect your goodness. May it be full of your fruit, and may it yield a large crop for your glory. You bring pure and passionate love, deep and abiding joy, powerful and persistent peace, relentless and gracious patience, unfailing and glorious kindness, indescribable goodness, and forever faithfulness. What you do is always good, always pure, and always builds me up.

I offer you access to every part of my heart and life. Oh, how I long to know your goodness in the details of my life! I am grateful that you are as present with me in the mundane as you are in moments of breakthrough. Your mercy is cultivating a garden in me as you tend to me with your presence.

I yield to the Holy Spirit in all areas. He is working in me to produce a bounty of his fruit. I will see where he is already working as I look for the evidence of love, joy, peace, patience, kindness, goodness, and faithfulness.

Every Morning

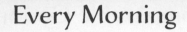

Lord, every morning you hear my voice.
Every morning, I tell you what I need,
and I wait for your answer.

PSALM 5:3 NCV

Lord, thank you for hearing my voice whenever I talk to you. Every morning and every moment, as I tell you what I need, I wait for your answer. In this give and take, this beautiful conversation in fellowship with your Spirit, I learn to rely more on your wisdom than my own understanding.

I won't stop coming to you every time I think of you. You are my hope, and the source of my joy. You are my strength and my purpose. Everything I need finds its true and lasting fulfillment in you. I will come to you before I turn anywhere else for answers. You are my counselor, my leader, and my provider. Thank you!

I declare that every moment I turn to the Lord and every prayer I pray is met by the loving willingness of God. He answers me, he communes with me, and he leads me. I will keep turning to him.

Greater Hope

We glory in our sufferings, because we know that suffering produces perseverance; perseverance character; and character, hope.

ROMANS 5:3-4 NIV

Persistent One, thank you for the greater hope that is available even in my darkest moments. No suffering is too great a burden to bear, for it is not the end. Use my tender and vulnerable moments to produce something beautiful for your kingdom, Lord.

When I suffer, I learn perseverance. Through perseverance, my character and compassion are strengthened. Through character development, there is hope for more in your kingdom. You never stop working in mercy, and you don't ever abandon me in my troubles. Thank you for your persistent presence that guides, shapes, and builds me up in your love. I depend on you.

No matter how discouraged I may feel at any given moment, there is more hope in Christ. There is more joy, more peace, and more life. There is always more. I press into him, and I invite his abundance to overwhelm my lack.

Promised Comfort

"Blessed are those who mourn,
for they shall be comforted."

MATTHEW 5:4 ESV

Comforter, I have known grief, and I know that I will again. Though it is painful, it is an invitation to expand as I move through it. Your love meets me in my mourning and comforts me. You do not snap your fingers and command me to step of my grief. You know that it is a path to be walked, and you are my constant companion through it.

Even when darkness shrouds my understanding of your expansive mercy, you are still with me. You are still sowing seeds of kindness as I walk in the wilderness. I lean on your love, and I depend on the support of your presence. When I can't move, carry me. Tucked into your side, I know that you will keep me safe and get me through this.

I will not run away from my grief. I will walk through it with the God of comfort as my companion. I will get through it, and I will know greater love because of the depths of my loss.

Seal of Hope

This is no empty hope, for God himself is the one who has prepared us for this wonderful destiny. And to confirm this promise, he has given us the Holy Spirit, like an engagement ring, as a guarantee.

2 Corinthians 5:5 tpt

Wonderful One, thank you for your Spirit who is the seal of your promised return. I have tasted and seen the goodness of your presence through fellowship with your Holy Spirit, and I long for more. You have revealed your character and your faithfulness through communion from Spirit to spirit.

What a wonderful and glorious mystery it is to know you! It is a holy pursuit be known by you and to seek after your heart. You called me out from the tyranny of the mundane into the glorious hope of your kingdom. I am undone by your faithful love in my life.

I have a full and expectant hope in Jesus. The Spirit is the fullness of God's presence, and he is with me now. I will feast on his presence and grow to know him more.

Gentle Strength

"Blessed are the gentle,
for they shall inherit the earth."

MATTHEW 5:5 NASB

Good Father, I love that Jesus represented your love not only in power but also in tenderness. I want to cultivate gentleness as a strength in my life without fear of being walked on or preyed upon. You have said, "Blessed are the gentle, for they shall inherit the earth." I want to live with calm kindness that pursues what is right in all things. I want to live a life of love that does not shout but displays the power of tenderness.

Compassion is gentle. It meets us where we are. I want to express compassion to others in the same way and without the desire to control or manipulate. You are so much better in your love than I could ever be, yet I long to be more like you. Help me keep my priorities straight.

I declare that gentleness is a strength and tenderness is valuable. I will not bolster myself in self-protection and become hardened to those who are hurting. I will remain soft as God's love keeps my heart in perfect peace.

Unashamed

Hope does not put us to shame, because God's love
has been poured into our hearts through the Holy Spirit
who has been given to us.

ROMANS 5:5 ESV

Holy Spirit, pour your love into my heart in greater
measure today. I know that there is no lack in you. There
is no draught in my Father's kingdom. Fill me up with
the resources of your endless mercy. Flood me with the
measures of your generous grace. Hope in you will always
be fruitful, so I will not give up hope.

I offer you the places that are dry, cracked, and desperate
for a fresh touch of your presence. Meet me, Lord. Do not
turn away. Come closer, and may I feast on the abundance
of your love. I need you!

*There is no lack of love in the fellowship of the Holy Spirit.
There is only abundance: more than enough for all I need,
all I hope for, and all that I don't even know to ask for.*

Active Trust

If you bow low in God's awesome presence,
he will eventually exalt you as you leave the timing
in his hands.

1 PETER 5:6 TPT

Glorious God, your presence leaves me astounded and awe-struck. As my perspective broadens in the light of your life, I feel time slow down and every sense come alive. Refresh my heart in you hope today. Revive my soul in your life-giving radiance. I humble myself before you as I long for the satisfaction of your presence to fill my weary heart and lift my burdens.

I trust you with the timing of all my hopes, dreams, and plans. I trust you with my longings. I won't stop the work that you have given me to do, but I will stop trying to control what it must look like. You are better than I am and your ways higher than my own. Your understanding takes everything that I can't see into account. I trust your timing.

I will remain humble before the Lord and trust that he will continue to be faithful. I trust his timing more than my own, and I let go of the need to control my future.

The Feast

"Blessed are those who hunger and thirst for righteousness, for they will be filled."

MATTHEW 5:6 NRSV

Lord, I hunger and thirst for you like a deer pants for the water on a hot day. I long for a fresh drink from your fountain. I long to taste and see your goodness once more. You are righteousness embodied, and I long for you. I'm grateful that you invite all those who seek after you to the banqueting table of your presence. There is a feast waiting for those who would come.

Today I come with all my faults and flaws. I lay aside every worry and every pressing matter to turn to you now. In this moment, I turn my attention fully to you. Please fill me with your life-giving love once again.

Whatever we thirst and hunger for, that we will seek. I hunger and thirst for God's presence more than anything else. I pursue his wisdom, his comfort, and his love. I know that I will be filled as he meets me with the abundance of his Spirit.

Give Away Stress

Pour out all your worries and stress upon him and leave them there, for he always tenderly cares for you.

1 PETER 5:7 TPT

Loving Lord, you clearly see the weight of my worries, and you know the burdens I carry. I don't want to carry them on my own any longer. I offer you all my worries and all my stress; I pour it all out to you. I will leave them there, and you will fill the empty space in me with your love.

I know that I was not meant to carry the weight of the world on my shoulders. It is not my responsibility to be perfect. It is not my duty to cover everyone else's weakness with my strength. I get to feast and fuel up on your love, and you take the heaviness and give me your light load. Thank you for reprieve, relief, and refreshment in your presence.

I don't have to carry the weight of my stress anymore! I declare that I give it all to God, and I leave it with him. I trust him to do what I could never do on my own. I know that he is faithful, true, and good.

Merciful and True

"Blessed are the merciful,
for they shall receive mercy."

MATTHEW 5:7 NASB

Merciful One, I want to look more like you when I interact with people. I want to be transformed into your image in every area of my life. I recognize that your mercy extends toward me in abundance, and it is this mercy that allows me to offer mercy to myself and to others.

There is so much love! There is so much grace! There is so much freedom in your presence. I trust you to deal justice, and I partner with your purposes. I will extend love where I am tempted to step back in pride. I will extend the benefit of the doubt and send forth compassion. At the same time, I will hold the boundaries I need to support myself and others in love. Thank you for your help in this as in all areas of my life. I surrender to you.

God has been merciful to me, and he continues to be. I will not withhold mercy when it is in my power to offer it. I will give mercy to myself in my own imperfections and trauma responses as well as to others in theirs. God is mighty in mercy.

Covered by Covenant

I know that you will welcome me into your house,
for I am covered by your covenant of mercy and love.
So I come to your sanctuary with deepest awe
to bow in worship and adore you.

PSALM 5:7 TPT

Promise Keeper, thank you for your faithfulness. You never fail, and I know that you never will. You are faithful and true, and you follow through on your Word. I am covered by your covenant of mercy and love, and I know that you will welcome me into your kingdom when I cross from the temporary to the eternal.

I come before you with deep awe and adoration to worship you in spirit and in truth. You are my God, and I look to you more than I look to any other. You are my hope, and all my longings are fulfilled in you.

God's covenant is his forever vow. He can't be talked out of it, and his mercy will never waver. I am covered by his covenant of love, and I will never be without it. I will live with confidence, and I will worship him for his unending goodness.

Undying Love

Christ proved God's passionate love for us by dying in our place while we were still lost and ungodly!

ROMANS 5:8 TPT

Christ, thank you for the passion of your love that led you to come to earth clothed in humanity. You took on flesh and bones; you limited yourself to our experience. You started out as a babe and grew in both understanding and authority. You did not count your own life as too great when you considered us.

I can never thank you enough or pour out enough love to repay you, but you don't require repayment. You just want a relationship with me. I am so alive in you! Thank you, Jesus! Thank you for breaking the curse of sin and death that kept the world in cycles of shame, fear, and lack. You are the abundant one, and you have given humanity abundant life in the resurrection power of your sacrifice.

I declare that God's passionate love is worth my submission, my trust, and my awe. I will worship him, for he is better than the best. He is full of loyal love, integrity, and power. I yield my life and love to him.

November

Be faithful to pray as
intercessors who are fully alert
and giving thanks to God.

COLOSSIANS 4:2 TPT

Children of Light

Once you were full of darkness, but now you have light from the Lord. So live as people of light! For this light within you produces only what is good and right and true.

EPHESIANS 5:8-9 NLT

Radiant One, I know what it's like to live in darkness, but I also know what it's like to live in your light. Your radiance shines from everything you do. You are rich in mercy, abundant in grace, and never-ending in loyal kindness. You are full of truth, wisdom, and relief.

I will live in the light and not in the shadows. I will live with love as my motivation and my motto. Your laid-down love shows me how to extend and expand in compassion. Your path is not easy, and not many choose to walk it all the way, but it is simple. The path of love is full of your light. I am yours, and I live with your light alive in me. You will show me the way as I move in you.

I declare that the light of love is my guiding force, my heart's motivation, and my holy hope. I am a child of the living God, and I am full of the light of his mercy. I will let my light shine bright.

Never Disgraced

The LORD God helps me,
Therefore, I am not disgraced;
Therefore, I have set my face like flint,
And I know that I will not be ashamed.

ISAIAH 50:7 NASB

Deliverer, with you as my help, I will not be disgraced. I trust you with my worries, the unknowns of my future, and the care of those I love. Lead me with your strong right hand. Keep me on the path of your light so that I do not stray from your loyal love. I will persevere in you while knowing that your mercy is stronger than the threats of the corrupt. Your justice will shine like the dawn, and you will make every wrong thing right.

You will do it! Why should I be afraid of what tomorrow will bring when you are faithful and true? You will not lead me into disgrace? I trust you.

I will not be ashamed as I pursue the Lord. I will not be ashamed of him, for he is not ashamed of me. I will rise up with wings like an eagle, and I will continue to receive his help whenever I need it.

Great Compassion

Have mercy on me, O God,
because of your unfailing love.
Because of your great compassion,
blot out the stain of my sins.

PSALM 51:1 NLT

Merciful Father, you are full of unfailing love. How could I begin to thank you for meeting me with generous mercy every time I turn to you? I lay out all my failures before you. Bolster me in your love and wipe away my guilt with your compassion. There is no one better than you. You remove the culpability of my sin as far as the east is from the west. Your forgiveness does not hold anything against me.

Even as I walk out the consequences of poor choices, I know that your mercy brings redemption. You will give me the strength to keep moving in your love, and you will restore what I could not on my own. Thank you.

When I am forgiven by God, I am fully forgiven. I will not hold against myself what God does not hold against me. I will walk in love and seek restoration with others with the freedom and confidence of his help.

All I Have

My sacrifice, O God, is a broken spirit;
a broken and contrite heart you, God, will not despise.

PSALM 51:17 NIV

All I have, Lord, I give to you. I don't have much to offer, but what I do have is yours. When all I have to give is a broken and contrite heart, you receive it lovingly. Revive me in your mercy again. I will surrender to your ways.

I have tried my best to live rightly, and I am far from perfect. I want to live for your satisfaction and not my own. I don't want to ignore what you are doing, for you are rich in love and always working miracles of mercy in the world. Fill my life with your Spirit fruit and grow a glorious garden of redemption in me. I am yours, Lord. All I have is yours.

I will not hide my weakness from God. Today I give him my wounded and broken heart; I know he will restore me in his love and make me whole. He is better than any other.

Beautiful Savior

He was pierced for our rebellion, crushed for our sins.
He was beaten so we could be whole. He was whipped
so we could be healed.

ISAIAH 53:5 NLT

Lord Jesus, it is difficult to meditate on what you went
through in the hours before your crucifixion. It is too
terrible to think about, but it is the revelation of love's
lengths to save us. Thank you for your sacrifice. Thank you
for enduring the unthinkable so that we could know the
fullness of the Father through you.

Your death was not the end of the story. Your resurrection
power is what makes me come alive in you! I am in awe of
the tenacity of your mercy; I am undone by the passion of
your love. Thank you for doing what none of us could to
give us freedom in you. Thank you.

*Jesus took every curse upon himself so that we wouldn't
have to live under its weight. I am alive in his love, and he
has taken away the weight of my sin.*

Every Burden

Give your burdens to the LORD,
and he will take care of you.
He will not permit the godly to slip and fall.

PSALM 55:22 NLT

Lord, there are times when I don't know how to give you the burdens that weigh down my soul. In my heartbreak and confusion, I don't know how to separate the weight from my pain. Still, I offer it to you. Take care of me, Lord. Tend to me as a mother tends to her sick child. Hold me up and carry me when I can't move myself at all.

I know that you aren't going anywhere. Your love is safe, persistent, and pure. Meet me with the liquid mercy of your presence and care for me in ways that I can't. Thank you for your constancy; thank you for rest in your peace.

The Lord watches over me. He cares for me, and he heals me. I now offer him the heaviness of my burdens and welcome his help.

Higher Wisdom

"As the heavens are higher than the earth,
so are My ways higher than your ways,
and My thoughts than your thoughts."

ISAIAH 55:9 NKJV

Great God, I am so grateful for the reminder that your ways are higher than our own. Your thoughts are better than our thoughts. As I look to the sky and consider what lies beyond my sight, I remind my soul that your love is larger than the expanse of the universe. Your mercy is everywhere. Your grace is always present. Your understanding is greater than the most astute minds on this earth. The breadth of your wisdom is larger than our little world can contain.

What a relief this is! I can trust you with all my questions, and I can come to you with my confusion. Show me a glimpse of your perspective and instruct me with your insights.

No one knows more than the Lord. His wisdom is unmatched; it takes everything into account. He is not stumped by my problems. He is never at a loss about what to do. I will trust him and follow his ways.

Lay It All Out

In the day that I'm afraid,
I lay all my fears before you
and trust in you with all my heart.

PSALM 56:3 TPT

Mighty One, I can't pretend to not be afraid when fear constricts my chest and pushes me in hasty directions to protect myself. I don't want to be ruled by fear; I want your peace. When I am afraid, I lay all my fears before you. I won't keep them to myself or try to manage them. I offer them all to you, and I choose to trust in your unfailing love. I will wait for your peace to fill my soul. I will wait on you.

You are my confidence and my sure help in times of trouble. You move with clarity and assurance. Move on my behalf, Lord. Give me courage to follow through on your wisdom. Whatever comes, I will take your hand and offer you everything in my heart and mind.

I will not keep my fears hidden. I will not just try to cope with anxiety on my own. I will lay it all out before God. I depend on his help, and I will reach out for support where I can. I trust the Lord.

Astonishing Faithfulness

Your love is so extravagant it reaches to the heavens,
Your faithfulness so astonishing it stretches to the sky!

PSALM 57:10 TPT

Faithful One, there will never come a day when your faithfulness won't be on display. You are working your mercy in the world even now. You are moving in my life even when I can't sense it. Your extravagant love doesn't miss a moment or a mark. You are abounding in love, and you are overwhelmingly good in your compassion.

Reveal your loyal love to me in new ways today. Give me eyes to see where you are. Give me ears to hear what you are saying over my life and over those around me. Mold my heart; transform it in your presence. You are more wonderful than I can comprehend, but I long to know you more.

I declare that the extravagant love of the Lord does not pass over me. It covers me entirely. It is my source of life, breath, and very good thing I have known. I worship the Lord, for he is unfailing in love.

I Will Sing

I will sing of Your power;
Yes, I will sing aloud of Your mercy in the morning;
For You have been my defense
And refuge in the day of my trouble.

PSALM 59:16 NKJV

Powerful God, as I meditate on your goodness, I will not hold back the song rising in my heart. I will sing aloud of your mercy. I will shout your praises, for you have been so very good to me, and you never give up on me.

Thank you for your unmitigated mercy. Thank you for your compassion. You have been my defense, and you will continue to be. You are my refuge in the day of trouble, and you are my shelter in times of uncertainty. You are the solid rock of my faith. You are powerful, and I trust that I will continue to see your goodness in my life and in the world around me.

I will sing to the Lord today, no matter how feeble or strong my voice is. I offer him the song of my heart, for he is my life source and strength.

Full of Justice

God is not unjust; he will not overlook your work and
the love that you showed for his sake in serving the
saints, as you still do.

HEBREWS 6:10 NRSV

God of Justice, you see everything offered to you. You
noticed every choice I made in love. You take it all into
account, and you haven't missed a thing. Even the things
that have gone completely unnoticed by others, you have
seen. You see it all.

I am submitted to you, Lord, and to your ways. I continue
to follow on your path of love even when it's tough to lay
down my preferences and offenses. I choose it because it
is your way. It is the better way. Fill me with your peace for
the journey. Fill me with your encouragement. Speak to me,
strengthen me, and walk with me through it all. You are my
vision, and I follow you.

*I choose to continue to surrender to the Lord and choose
love in all things. I trust that the Lord sees what I do and
that it matters to him. He will reward me for every act of
compassion. He is just, and he will have the last say in all
things.*

Under Grace

Sin shall no longer be your master,
because you are not under the law, but under grace.

ROMANS 6:14 NIV

Gracious God, I am grateful that sin is not my master.
Shame is not my leader. Fear is not my commander.
Guilt is not the one who directs me. You are. Your grace
has met me with the generosity of your love. You have
overwhelmed me with your kindness and drawn me to
refreshing waters of reviving in your presence. You have
removed the stain of my mistakes, and you do not hold my
past against me. You have liberated me in your love; you
have set me free in your saving grace.

Thank you for this gift. Remove the remnants of my guilt.
Blow away the dust of fearful narratives. There is relief in
your presence, and I long for the presence of your Spirit in
mine. Do it again, Lord.

There is no condemnation for me in Christ. He loves me
fully, sets me free in his mercy, and fills me with his peace.
I am alive under grace's liberation over my life.

True Trust

Teach those who are rich in this world not to be proud and not to trust in their money, which is so unreliable. Their trust should be in God, who richly gives us all we need for our enjoyment.

1 TIMOTHY 6:17 NLT

Wise One, I know that physical resources come and go. Money can get me to some places, but it is unreliable and not worth building my life on. I don't want my life to be under the pressure of achieving or maintaining a lifestyle of leisure. I want to live for what matters, to build my life upon your love that is always abundant, always constant, and never changes value.

I trust you and your teachings more than I trust what I have or could have. I will not despise or love money. I will see it as the tool it is. I choose to keep first things first and stay rooted in your steady mercy.

True trust does not come with having enough or doing enough. There will always be unforeseen challenges. True trust is developed in relationship, and the living God is unchanging in mercy. He is a rock-solid foundation that will never be moved. I trust him more than any other.

Hidden in Faithfulness

It is impossible for God to lie for we know that his promise and his vow will never change! And now we have run into his heart to hide ourselves in his faithfulness. This is where we find his strength and comfort, for he empowers us to seize what has already been established ahead of time—an unshakeable hope.

HEBREWS 6:18 TPT

Constant One, I am so grateful that you are better than humanity. You never tell a lie, you never recant your words, and you do not change your mind. You are consistent in mercy, you are relentless in kindness, and you are victorious in reigning justice.

Today I run into your heart and hide myself in your faithfulness. I will keep on running to you, for you never change. When my heart is upset by unforeseen hurts and betrayals, you remain constant in abounding love. You have not changed. In your heart, I find your strength and comfort, and you empower me to seize the unshakeable hope of your promises.

I declare that I will run into God's heart whenever I think of it. I will hide myself in his faithfulness. I will remind myself of his goodness. Over and over again, until it's as natural as breathing, I will do it.

Anchor of Hope

We have this hope as an anchor for the soul,
firm and secure.

HEBREWS 6:19 NIV

Jesus, the anchor of my hope is tied to you. My prayers, combined with yours, form the rope that tethers me to the unshakeable hope of your kingdom where you reign in grace and truth. You present my case before the Father just as any high priest does. You have gone before me, and you have paved the way.

Though the winds of testing toss me around, I know that the anchor of my hope is secure in your love. It will not be moved. You won't let go. Fill me with the strength and comfort of your presence and calm my worried heart with your peace. I trust you.

I declare that the hope of my salvation can't be moved, stolen, or taken from me. I will be found firmly established in the kingdom of Christ, for he is my King and my leader. I have given him my allegiance.

Be Blessed

The LORD bless you and keep you;
the LORD make his face to shine upon you,
and be gracious to you;
the LORD lift up his countenance upon you,
and give you peace.

NUMBERS 6:24-26 NRSV

Lord, I receive this ancient blessing today. I recite it over my own soul. I know that there is power in speaking the words, and I believe there is strength in a blessing. As I read this prayer, will you fill me with the nearness of your presence? Meet me with the power of your Spirit and rise up within me.

As I go about my day, show me others for whom I can also pray this blessing. I love partnering with you, and I love seeing you move in other people's hearts and lives. Encourage me so that I may be an encouragement.

I declare that I will freely bless those in my life. Even those who curse me, I will choose to bless as Jesus taught us to do. I believe that there is greater freedom in a blessing than there is in an offended heart.

Evidence All Around

"Look at the birds. They don't plant or harvest or store food in barns, for your heavenly Father feeds them. And aren't you far more valuable to him than they are? Can all your worries add a single moment to your life?"

MATTHEW 6:26 NLT

Heavenly Father, as I consider how nature cycles and animals find their food and shelter, I am encouraged to trust that you will care for and provide for me in the same way. You are good, you are faithful, and you are constant. Worrying about what may or may not happen won't help me at all. It will only disconnect me from the present.

I want to be fully involved and engaged in today. When I start to get distracted by anxiety, will you help me refocus? I know that as I meditate on you, I can focus on the now. I can slow down and step into the moment with deep breathing. I will find stillness in you.

I choose to not worry about tomorrow. I choose to enjoy the present. I choose to fully engage in my relationships, to do what I know to do today, and to leave the rest in God's hands.

First and Foremost

"Seek the Kingdom of God above all else, and live righteously, and he will give you everything you need."

MATTHEW 6:33 NLT

God, it is your kingdom that I seek above all else. I want to live rightly, to choose your love in all things, and to live without regret. I am submitted to your will and ways. Give me insight to see where cultural conditioning and empty traditions have taken the place of your mercy. I don't want to search for sameness instead of radical love. I want to risk looking foolish to others if it means that I am following your ways.

Jesus, I know that your standards are not the standards I would choose. They are not even the same standards I have been taught. Lead me, Lord, in your everlasting path. I put you above every leader, every lover, and every other figurehead in my life. Your ways are better.

The ways of God's kingdom are not the ways of this world. And yet, they are so much better. I choose Jesus' way. I choose to follow his example. I will trust him to provide all I need.

Promised Acceptance

"All that the Father gives me will come to me, and whoever comes to me I will never cast out."

JOHN 6:37 ESV

Jesus, thank you for your unfailing mercy. It invites me in and does not push me away. In your mercy, I find myself seeking you and longing for your presence to fill and fuel my life. I am confident that I am here because you called me. I have answered your call, and my heart responds by running into your heart. I am yours, I am submitted to you, and I trust you to keep me close.

Though others put conditions on their love, you don't. What purity of affection! What kindness and liberty! Thank you. Help me to reflect your love in the ways I interact with people in my life. Whom you do not reject, may I not reject either. Your mercy always beckons, always gathers, always extends.

I come alive in the love of Jesus, and I am free in his opinion of me. He is better than any other, and I will continue to press into knowing. I will reflect his mercy in my daily life.

Choose Forgiveness

"Judge not, and you will not be judged;
condemn not, and you will not be condemned;
forgive, and you will be forgiven."

LUKE 6:37 ESV

Lord, it goes against my natural tendency to forgive those who don't seem to care whether they've hurt others. It is difficult to extend mercy to the arrogant. It's not easy to withhold judgment from those who so clearly wrong others. Still, your love for all is strong, it is pure, and it is greater than my leanings.

Give me strength to forgive. Heal my heart. Give me courage to stand for accountability when it is necessary. Forgiveness does not mean allowing powerful people to prey on the vulnerable. As for me, I will not let the bitter root of judgment, condemnation, or unforgiveness grow in the soil of my heart. Help me, Jesus.

I declare that it is better to forgive than to hold on to offense. I will release those that have hurt me while also not shrinking away from the truth. I choose mercy.

Overflowing Grace

"Give, and you will receive. You will be given much.
Pressed down, shaken together, and running over,
it will spill into your lap. The way you give to others
is the way God will give to you."

LUKE 6:38 NCV

Generous One, I follow your example today. You freely give
out of the abundance of your love, and with your mercy as
my source, I will freely give too. Every time I do, you fill me
up afresh. When I choose generosity, you reward me with
more than I had before.

I trust you to care for me, to instruct me in your wisdom,
and to continue to raise me up in your kingdom ways.
I recognize that generosity is a value of your kingdom,
so I will not ignore its importance in my life. Increase my
understanding of your greatness as I practice extending
mercy in practical and powerful ways. Thank you for
opportunities to do this today.

*God is gracious, generous, and more able than I realize. I
will not hold back in fear. Instead, I will give freely in the
wisdom of Christ. I know that God will meet me there.*

Good to Do

Remember that the Lord will reward each one of us
for the good we do.

EPHESIANS 6:8 NLT

Mighty God, I know that there is good to do today.
There are opportunities to meet others with practical
compassion. There are invitations to slow down and meet
people where they are. May I not be too busy with my own
agenda that I miss opportunities to extend kindness to
others.

Spirit, you have my permission to get my attention at any
point today. Direct my focus to where yours lies. Show me
where I can make a difference. Reveal where I already have
tools to help others. I yield to you, Lord. I want to partner
with your heart and power. I will look for ways to bless
others with kindness, consistency, and follow-through.

*I declare that my actions matter as much as my word. I will
follow through on promises I make, and I will take time to
slow down and compassionately connect with others today.*

He Already Knows

"Your Father already knows what you need
before you ask him."

MATTHEW 6:8 TPT

Father, I have so much on my heart. You see it all already.
You already know what I want to ask you. What a relief to
know you are compassionate and receive me with open
arms. I lay it all out before you now and ask that, more
than anything, you would meet me with the power of your
presence right here where I am.

Lift the heavy burdens I've been holding as I offer them
to you. Work out what I can't control. Fill me with grace,
wisdom, and compassion. Imbue me with strength and
courage to face what is daunting. I trust you. I depend
on you. Please bow away my expectations with your
exceeding goodness.

*God is a father, and he is a good one at that. He never turns
me away in my time of need. He offers me all I need. I will
not hold back a thing from him today.*

Don't Quit

Let's not get tired of doing what is good.
At just the right time we will reap a harvest of blessing
if we don't give up.

GALATIANS 6:9 NLT

Unfailing One, you know how wearying life can feel at times. You have lived it. Give me your divine perspective that breathes renewed expectation within my soul. I invite your Spirit to fill me afresh today with the power of your presence. Empower me with your peace, joy, love, and hope; I need them all.

With your grace and strength alive within me, I will keep on persevering in good. I will keep doing what I know to do. I will keep following your wisdom. I will keep going. I trust the harvest is coming when all the hard work of endurance will pay off. I trust you, Lord.

I trust that as I keep persevering in love, I will taste the abundance of its harvest in time. I declare that God's ways are worth it. He will fill me with joy, peace, and hope as I follow him.

Praise for Despair

To all who mourn in Israel, he will give a crown of beauty for ashes, a joyous blessing instead of mourning, festive praise instead of despair. In their righteousness, they will be like great oaks that the LORD has planted for his own glory.

ISAIAH 61:3 NLT

Lord, I cling to your promised and coming redemption. I hold on to the hope of your healing within my soul, body, and life. You are the one who trades beauty for ashes, a joy for my mourning, and praise in place of my despair. I give you my weakness, my soul's weariness, and my heartache. Please give me the riches of your kingdom in return. Tend to me, cultivate me, and build me up in your strong love.

I want my life to reflect the power of your restoration and redemption. I need you to do what I can't even hope to ask for right now. Do much more than I can imagine with the power of your resurrection life in me.

Despair is not my inheritance, and disappointment is not the end of my road. There is more joy, more hope, more praise, more beauty, and more goodness coming. There is more here, now, in his presence.

Standing in Wait

I am standing in absolute stillness,
silent before the one I love,
waiting as long as it takes for him to rescue me.
Only God is my Savior, and he will not fail me.

PSALM 62:5 TPT

God my Savior, I stand before you in absolute stillness now. I quiet my heart and mind before you. You are the one I love, and you are the one I rely on for help. You are my only Savior, my only true hope, and my deliverer. Don't fail me, Lord!

Just as you answered the prophets and the psalmists who cried out to you, you will answer me. I will not move until you speak. I will not move on until you come to my rescue. I stand in wait, my heart tuned to you and my soul standing at attention. Come, Lord.

I don't need to rush into my day or into any situation without the Lord's help. I choose to wait on him today and trust him to speak and come through for me.

The Potter's Hand

O LORD, you are our Father;
we are the clay, and you are our potter;
we are all the work of your hand.

ISAIAH 64:8 ESV

Creator, you are both the one who formed me and my Father. You dreamt me up in your imagination before you breathed life into my flesh and bones. You knew what you were doing when you made me, and I will not despise my frailty or my gifts.

I am glad that there is intention behind every life. There is beauty in all you have created, and that includes me. You are the potter, and I am your clay. You have formed me, and you continue to form me. Have your way in my life, for I trust that you always know what's best.

I declare that the Lord knew what he was doing when he created me, and he called it good. I am firm in my identity as a dearly loved child. I will live in the freedom of that confidence and trust him to continue his mercy in my life.

Motherly Comfort

"As a mother comforts her child,
so I will comfort you."

ISAIAH 66:13 NIV

Comforter, wrap around me with the warmth of your presence. Embrace me with your love and comfort the pain in my soul. Soothe my worried heart, speak your life-giving truth over my circumstances, and reveal your unchanging perspective that about my worth.

I need your comfort. I need your real help. Today I pour out all my disappointments, heartaches, and fears. I will let myself feel the depth of loss as you hold me close. I trust that you are closer than my breath and that you are supporting me even now. Be near, Lord, in tangible love. Be near and relieve the pain I am in.

The love of God is not distant, and it is not cold. It is as close as a mother's touch. I am held, comforted, and revived by the source of love. Wrapped in the merciful kindness of God's heart, I am safe, and I can heal.

Everyone Has a Place

Father to the fatherless, defender of widows—
this is God, whose dwelling is holy.

PSALM 68:5 NLT

Defender, you never overlook the vulnerable. You always cover and protect those who have no one else to look out for them. You are a father to the fatherless, and you are the defender of widows. You are holy, just, and true, and you will never change. Your love is not weak; your mercy is stronger than the grave. Yes, it is more powerful than death!

There is no curse, no corruption, no evil in this world that can overcome your powerful love. Nothing can separate us from it. No one and nothing can come between us and your love. I will live with eyes open to see where I can partner with your heart. I will join you in providing for those without homes, defending the vulnerable, and standing for your justice.

God does not overlook anyone's dilemmas. He does not leave the vulnerable to fight their own battles, and I won't either. I will reach out in love, stand up for justice, and welcome the hurting. God's love does not exclude anyone, and neither will I.

Humble Vision

The humble will see their God at work and be glad.
Let all who seek God's help be encouraged.

PSALM 69:32 NLT

God, I humble my heart before you now. I don't want pride to keep me from hearing and following your wisdom. I don't want offense to keep me from the benefits of your love. I don't want to stay stuck in fear because I think it's safer than trusting you in the great unknown.

I'm seeking your help today as I do so often. I'm tired of trying to make my own way. I'm weary of trying to control what I can't possibly manage. I humbly submit to you. I know I can do my part and leave the rest with you. Give me gladness for my frustration, joy for my confusion, and peace for my anxiety. I know there is more goodness in you than I have already tasted.

It is worth it to humble myself before God and others. I will not let pride make me feel more important than anyone else. I can be strong and humble, wise and compassionate, shrewd and forgiving.

December

The LORD is close to everyone
who prays to him,
to all who truly pray to him.

PSALM 145:18 NCV

Healing Will Come

"If My people who are called by My name humble
themselves and pray and seek My face and turn from
their wicked ways, then I will hear from heaven,
will forgive their sin and will heal their land."

2 CHRONICLES 7:14 ESV

Messiah, I will not waste another moment in excusing my
lack of faith, my lack of wonder, and my self-protective
responses. I humble myself before you now, praying openly
and vulnerably, and I seek your face as if my very life
depends on it. My life does depend on it! I turn from my
selfish ways and run to you, holy and merciful God.

Forgive me for my wandering ways and bring me back on
to the path of your living love. Heal the decimated areas of
my heart and life. Bring redemption and restoration. I yield
to you.

*The Lord hears those who call on him. He answers those
who turn to him. I choose to submit myself to him, for I
believe that he is good, merciful, powerful, and true. I trust
him more than I trust myself.*

Springs of Water

"The Lamb in the midst of the throne will be their shepherd, and he will guide them to springs of living water, and God will wipe away every tear from their eyes."

REVELATION 7:17 ESV

Lamb of God, you are my shepherd. You are my loving leader. Guide me to the springs of your living water and refresh me in the beauty of your presence. I am so very weary of this world. There is too much heaviness to bear when I try to do it alone. There is too much information, too much evil, just too much.

Lead me to the refreshing fountains of your mercy and revive me in your pure joy. In your presence, I get a glimpse of the age to come, an age where pain, injustice, and loss will be a memory. I know that you will wipe every tear from our eyes. Even now, Lord, meet me in my sorrow and wipe my tears.

Jesus is my shepherd, and I trust him to give me all I need. I trust him to lead me into the goodness of his kingdom. I trust him to provide for me, lead me into rest, and care for my life. I lay down my worries and lean into his love today.

Once Again

Once again you will have compassion on us.
You will trample our sins under your feet
and throw them into the depths of the ocean!

MICAH 7:19 NLT

Compassionate One, thank you for the resurrection power of your life in mine. Thank you for the unending mercy I find in your presence. Thank you for your Spirit who ministers comfort, strength, and courage to my soul whenever I need it. You are better than I can describe.

Once again, draw me close in your kindness. Fill me up with the pure pleasure of your affection. There is nothing better than knowing you. I have found fullness of freedom, joy, and hope in you. I am so very loved by you, and I love you freely in return. Thank you for your new mercies every morning.

I declare that this moment is an opportunity to be met by the overwhelming compassion of God's heart. He is not angry or disappointed. He is full of love that will revive my soul, correct my wrongs, and cultivate growth in my life.

More than Able

He is able, once and forever, to save those who come to God through him. He lives forever to intercede with God on their behalf.

HEBREWS 7:25 NLT

Jesus Christ, you are my Savior. You are the way, the truth, and the life. You are the open door to the Father, and I freely enter in by your grace. There is fullness of joy in your presence; there is full acceptance in your Spirit. I am yours completely, Lord, and I rely on your help all the days of my life.

I believe that you are more than able to keep me secure in your love. You save all those who come to you. You offer your redemption to all who come to God through you. I don't hesitate to enter in. Thank you for your intercession, for your Spirit's help, and for the power of your relentless love. I belong to you.

I don't have to fear for my salvation when my life is yielded to Jesus. He is the King of kings and Lord of lords. He is the Savior of the world. He is my confidence, my strength, and my support. He is my everything.

Doors Opening

"Ask and it will be given to you;
seek and you will find;
knock and the door will be opened to you."

MATTHEW 7:7 NIV

Lord, only you know what resides deep within my heart.
Only you can see what I have been afraid to say out loud.
There are things that have felt too tender to verbalize, yet I
know that I can trust you with my most vulnerable longings.
I know that you are gentle with me, and you are patient.
Your love does not push me to my breaking point. When
it pushes me, I am swept up in a great river of your mercy,
and it is safe and secure. I am brought along by its current.

Your love doesn't look for ways to manipulate me into
submission. Your love doesn't seek to control me. Your
love sets me free! It is from this place of freedom I will pray
today and ask for the things on my heart.

*When I ask the Lord for anything, he hears me. He will not
withhold his goodness from me when it is in his power and
plan to give it. I will keep seeking, knocking, and pressing
into him, for he is the goodness I'm looking for.*

Know This

> "Know therefore that the LORD your God is God;
> he is the faithful God, keeping his covenant of love
> to a thousand generations of those who love him
> and keep his commandments."

DEUTERONOMY 7:9 NIV

Lord God, I know that you are faithful. You keep your covenant of love to a thousand generations and beyond. You do not change from dealing with me in mercy. I love you, and I have given you leadership of my life. I trust you to work all things together in your kindness for my good and for your ultimate glory. Weave the tattered threads of my brokenness into the wholeness of your mercy. Please do what only you can do.

As for me, I trust you. I trust you with my heart, my plans, and my well-being. I trust you to continue your goodness beyond me and my little life. I trust you to keep your covenant of love in the generations that overlap and follow. You are faithful, and that will never change.

I declare that the goodness of the Lord knows no end. Today is full of his kindness. His covenant of love is still working in my life, and my heart can rest in him.

No Judgment

There is therefore now no condemnation
for those who are in Christ Jesus.

ROMANS 8:1 ESV

Christ Jesus, thank you for taking the weight of my
shame and for making me blameless in the Father's sight.
Wrapped in your love, I am purified and free. Help me to
live with the confidence of your mercy as my foundation. I
don't want to shrink myself or others because of my ideas
about what you do or don't accept. In your mercy, every
wrong is made right. In your resurrection power, I find true
liberty to live like you exemplified.

I don't want to judge others for things that you have
forgiven me for. Give me grace to release unrealistic
expectations and to extend compassion and mercy. I want
a soft, warm heart instead of a cold one.

*What Jesus does not condemn, neither will I. I will live in
the confidence of Christ's mercy in my life, and I will extend
the power of that same mercy to others.*

Light of the World

"I am the light of the world.
Whoever follows me will not walk in darkness,
but will have the light of life."

JOHN 8:12 ESV

Jesus, you are the light of the world. You shine like the radiant sun. The shadows disappear in your light, and everything becomes clear. You burn off the fog of confusion with your presence. You open up possibilities I could not see without your help.

I follow you, Jesus, today and every day. You are the light of my life. Shine on areas of darkness in my life that I may not see. Light up the shadows so that I will know where you are even as you reveal where I am in you. I lean on your understanding, your help, and your presence to guide, preserve, and propel me. Shine on me, Lord.

The light of God shines in my darkest night and gives me vision to see what I could not understand without him. I will lean on his wisdom, press into his presence, and trust him above all others.

Spirit of Adoption

You have not received a spirit that makes you fearful slaves. Instead, you received God's Spirit when he adopted you as his own children. Now we call him, "Abba, Father."

ROMANS 8:15 NLT

Abba, I know that I can come to you freely and without fear in every moment. I choose to do that now. Thank you for receiving me with compassion. You know me better than anyone else does; you are my good, good Father. I am running into your embrace right now. I will not hold myself back, for you beckon me to come. You draw me in with kindness. You lure me with love. How could I stay away? Why would I choose to?

Speak to me, Father, as I run into your presence today. Hold me, reassure me, and teach me. I know that you meet me with abundance and intimate knowledge every time I turn to you. You do not hold a thing against me, but you will call me out in your wisdom. I am your child.

I will not let my experience with my own parents' failures keep me from coming to the Lord today. I know that he is perfect in love. He always knows what I need, and I will find satisfaction and relief in him.

Seek and Find

I will show my love to those who passionately love me.
For they will search and search continually until they
find me.

PROVERBS 8:17 TPT

Compassionate One, I am searching for more of you. I long
to find you in the details of my day. I want to see where
your mercy meets me in the dirt. Where you are, there is
holy ground. Even here, where I sit at this moment, you are
with me.

I don't have to look very hard to find you. Still, the hunger in
my soul is growing. My heart longs to be quenched by your
love. I love you, and I won't stop loving you. An even greater
truth is that you loved me first. Open my eyes to see where
your love is lurking. Increase my understanding so that I
may perceive the greatness of your kindness in my life.

*The Lord promises that he will be found by those who
hunger and thirst for him. I will be filled, and my thirst will
be satisfied by the living waters of his presence. Yes, Lord!*

Joy Will Return

He will once again fill your mouth with laughter
and your lips with shouts of joy.

JOB 8:21 NLT

Redeemer, I long for the days of easy laughter to return.
I want to be so in tune with your joy, so in touch with
your delight, that laughter comes quickly as the relief of
gladness floods my soul. I know that your joy is always
available and always near no matter how dry I've been
feeling.

Will you refresh me in the abundant pleasure of your love
today? I long for you more than I can express. Let hope rise
within me as you pour over my mind, heart, soul, and body
with your presence. You are my overwhelming goodness in
every season of the soul, and I know that you will not fail me.

*The Lord is my strength and my song. He is my deliverer
and my strong tower. He is my delight and my ultimate joy.
His generous love is mine! Today I will know the refreshing
relief of his presence with me.*

Spirit Strength

The Spirit helps us with our weakness. We do not know how to pray as we should. But the Spirit himself speaks to God for us, even begs God for us with deep feelings that words cannot explain.

ROMANS 8:26 NCV

Holy Spirit, I am grateful for your help in all things. I turn my attention to your nearness, and I ask for a fresh revelation of your power at work within me. Please meet with me. Expand my understanding in your wisdom. Reveal the strength of your tangible grace that renews my motivation and relieves my worries. You are better than an ideology, more powerful than wishful thinking, and more real than my fears.

Spirit, move within me and on my behalf with deep, inexpressible intercession. When I don't know how to pray, I know that you can read my feelings, my hopes, my disappointments, and my very soul. I trust you to express what I can't and to communicate it to the Father on my behalf.

I am not alone. I have the Spirit of God working within and around me. He is my help, my comfort, my strength, my joy, and so much more. I have all I need in him today.

All for Good

We know that for those who love God all things work together for good, for those who are called according to his purpose.

ROMANS 8:28 ESV

Lord, I trust that even what I can't understand is within the realm of your sovereignty. Though some things in the world are too awful, too tragic, and too traumatic, I do not believe that you are the cause of those things. You are merciful, and you meet us in the messes of our lives. You are the Redeemer, and you turn what could have destroyed us into pools for our healing.

As I rely more on you, I trust that you are making me whole in your love. You will not let a single thing go to waste in your mercy. You will restore what others have sought to destroy, and you will sow goodness into the wastelands of my journey.

I trust that God is not done working his miracles of mercy in my story. He is still active in my life, and he will turn my mourning into dancing. He will usher in seasons of plenty where his Spirit fruit is abundant and evident. I will praise him and trust him.

Abide in Truth

Jesus said to the Jews who had believed him, "If you abide in my word, you are truly my disciples, and you will know the truth, and the truth will set you free."

JOHN 8:31-32 ESV

Jesus, I am so grateful that there is promised freedom in your truth. I want to look for your liberating love in your Word and in my life. I will spend time in the gospels and fill up on your words. I will meditate on your living truth so that it transforms me from the inside out.

I believe you are who you say you are: you are the way, the truth, and the life. You are the Savior, you are good, and you are faithful. You are merciful, patient, kind, and just. You are the God who heals, the God who saves, and the God who redeems. You simply are! I will abide in your Word today. As I do, expand my knowledge of your goodness.

The Lord God is true, and he is full of life-giving love. I meditate on his Word today, and I will let it ring through my mind and heart throughout the day. I will be set free in his truth.

Loose Grasp

"If you try to hang on to your life, you will lose it. But if you give up your life for my sake and for the sake of the Good News, you will save it. And what do you benefit if you gain the whole world but lose your own soul?"

MARK 8:35-36 NLT

Lord God, I want to hold tightly to the things that last while keeping a loose grasp on the things that quickly fade. I don't want to count my life as too great a price to follow you. You are worthy of my days as much as you are the whole scope of my lifetime.

I know that devotion is made up of moments and the daily choices we make. Help me choose you. Help me choose your love, your compassion, and the benefit of others as much as I choose my own pleasure and preferences. I know that the lost are found in you. There is no one else like you.

My life has been transformed by the good news of the gospel, and I will not forget it. I will keep a loose grip on my plans and allow the Lord's compassion to guide me today.

Glorious Victory

Even in the midst of all these things, we triumph over them all, for God has made us to be more than conquerors, and his demonstrated love is our glorious victory over everything.

ROMANS 8:37 TPT

Great God, even in the midst of all my troubles and trials, you have made a way for me to overcome in your joy. You are the glorious victor over all. You are above my pain, my suffering, and my heartache, yet your mercy is with me through it all.

You have called me to be more than a conqueror through your living love. Your resurrection power is accessible to me today, and I will not forget it. You redeem what seems irredeemable. You breathe life into dry bones, and you melt the coldest hearts with the fire of your passion. Your extravagant love is my hope, my bread, and my everything. Fill me up once again. Love me to life in your presence so that I may raise up in your victory as a confident conqueror.

I am more than a conqueror through Christ. Whatever I face today, I face it with the power of his living love as my source. I come alive in his mercy over and over again.

Nothing in Creation

I am convinced that neither death nor life, neither angels nor demons, neither the present nor the future, nor any powers, neither height nor depth, nor anything else in all creation, will be able to separate us from the love of God that is in Christ Jesus our Lord.

ROMANS 8:38-39 NIV

Creator, I believe that you are the source of every living thing. You are the one who placed the stars in the sky and set the planets in motion. You created the cycles of life. Nothing exists outside of you and your loyal love.

Your Word says that you are love. Everything you do reflects your indescribably powerful mercy and kindness. Nothing in all creation, either above or below, can keep me from this love. Nothing from my past, present, or future can separate me from you. You are my source. You are my hope. You are my purpose. You are everything I need and so much more than I could expect to receive. You are overwhelmingly good, and I rely on you.

Nothing can separate me from the love of God in Christ. His goodness is at work in my life, and I know that his abundance is mine today. He does not give me scraps of love; he always gives a full portion.

Kindness and Honor

The LORD God is like a sun and shield;
the LORD gives us kindness and honor.
He does not hold back anything good
from those whose lives are innocent.

PSALM 84:11 NCV

Lord God, I know that when I take time to look at who you are, my heart is encouraged. You are faithful, you are true, and you are abundant in kindness. You offer me the same kindness and honor that you offer to any who look to you for help. Meet me with the generosity of your love today.

In my joy, you are present. In my need, you are present. You are my sun and shield. You shine light on the shadows and give me eyes to see. You wrap around me with the shield of your presence and give me insight into your kingdom ways as you cover me with your protective grace. I believe that you are generous; you will not hold back your goodness from me. I am yours, Lord.

The Lord offers me his kindness and honor. Where I would shrink in self-blame, he offers mercy. I will rise up in his living love and let his radiant glory shine on me.

Enriched by God

How enriched are they
who find their strength in the Lord;
within their hearts are the highways of holiness!

PSALM 84:5 TPT

Good Father, you know how much I rely on your grace and strength in my life. Though I can go a ways on my own, my resources wane. My hope depletes in times of testing. My resolve wavers when the winds of this world blow unrelentingly my way.

You, oh Lord, are my strength and my shield. You are the one who always offers an abundance of grace. There is nothing that you withhold from those who love and seek after you. Your mercy is powerful enough to break through the shame of my failures. It is large enough to redeem what I could never revive on my own. You are so much better than I could ever dream of being. I am enriched by you, Lord. My heart is yours.

The highways of holiness are not found in physical journeys. They are found in the paths we pave within our hearts. My heart is following the path of Christ's love, and I will not stop.

Abounding Passion

You, O Lord, are good and forgiving,
abounding in steadfast love to all who call upon you.

PSALM 86:5 ESV

Lord, how wonderfully good and forgiving you are. Your mercy is not weak. Your love is not frail. It is stronger than the grave. I want to live with the confidence of your love alive in me. I want to choose compassion instead of cold judgment. I want to choose mercy instead of apathy.

This is not easy. Choosing to engage in love is costly. You counted each of us worth that price. Why would I live to protect myself when your example is to lay down everything in the name of love? Though your steadfast love is not easy to emulate at all times, it is worth the cost. You are worth it! I call upon the name of the Lord who forgives my sin. I live in the light of your liberty and choose to follow your example.

The passion of the Lord is full of wisdom, strength, and hope. He is love incarnate. I will live with love as my motto as I interact with others today.

No Matter What

I will be strength to him
and I will give him my grace
to sustain him no matter what comes.

PSALM 89:21 TPT

Mighty God, thank you for the open-ended invitation of your unending grace. It is my sustenance in every season, in every time of need, and in every question. No matter what comes, you will be my strength. No matter what lies ahead, you offer me your grace. No matter what, you are with me.

I'm beyond thankful for this reminder today. Refresh my hope in you as your truth washes over me. Restore my peace as you expand your love within me. You are endlessly good. You are full of grace. I come to your waters and drink deeply of your present peace. I fill up on your truth.

The Lord promises to be my strength. No matter what, he offers his grace to sustain me. I will take him up on his offer today. I look to him for renewal and for the empowering grace to persevere in hope.

Trustworthy and True

Those who know your name trust in you,
for you, Lord, have never forsaken those who seek you.

PSALM 9:10 NIV

Faithful Father, I trust you to sustain me. I trust you to comfort me. I trust you to give me the strength to pursue your will and ways as I journey through this life. I trust you to never leave.

You said that you will never abandon those who look to you. I am looking to you right now, and I won't stop. I wait on you, trusting you to give me all I need. I will follow your mercy's ways rather than staying stuck in fear. When you urge me on, I will follow you. When you tell me to wait on your help, I will wait. Thank you for the fellowship of your Spirit. I trust you!

The Lord is trustworthy and true, and he will never change. Today I remind my soul of what he has already done in faithfulness. I will keep looking to him as I press into hope and persevere through all that comes my way.

It Is Possible

"Everything is possible
for one who believes."

MARK 9:23 NIV

Savior, you have given me more than I could ever repay.
You have opened the way to the fullness of the Father's
presence, and I enter in. I come close as you draw me in
with your Spirit. I hear your words of life: "Don't be afraid; I
am with you."

As you shower me with songs of love and rhythms of
life, I am swept up in your kindness and revived in hope. I
don't have to be perfect to be righteous. I am yours, and
I yield to your mercy that covers me. You have made the
impossible possible, and you will continue to move in ways
I can't imagine. You are better than the best days and
faithful in my worst days. I trust your Word; I trust your
presence. I trust your love. You have my heart, Lord, and I
won't take it back.

*The impossible becomes possible in the miraculous mercy
of God. What God says, he will do. What he promises, he
will fulfill. I will hold on to hope, and I will press into prayer
to know the incomparable power of God in my life.*

Wonderful Counselor

To us a child is born,
To us a son is given;
and the government shall be upon his shoulder,
and his name shall be called
Wonderful Counselor, Mighty God,
Everlasting Father, Prince of Peace.

ISAIAH 9:6 ESV

Mighty God, as I meditate on the humbling you took upon yourself, I am reminded of how mercy meets me now. You did not count your life and kingdom as too high a cost; you laid them aside for a time to show us what you're like. You, who knew no wrong or shame, took upon yourself my blame. I am free because you redeemed me.

I honor your life. I honor your death, and I honor your resurrection power. You are Wonderful Counselor, Mighty God, Everlasting Father, Prince of Peace, and so many other things. I remember who you were, and I remember that you never change. You are alive! You are still the same, and you will forever be.

Jesus humbled himself to show us the way to the Father. He gives us liberty and peace. He offers restoration. I honor him today, and I offer him my praise.

Share Freely

God is able to provide you with every blessing in abundance, so that by always having enough of everything, you may share abundantly in every good work.

2 CORINTHIANS 9:8 NRSV

Good Father, thank you for your plentiful mercy. You don't hold back any good thing from us. You are full of loyal love, overflowing in peace, and always abundant in joy. You see the areas of need in my life before I know to ask.

Today I'm asking for a tangible touch of your mercy to reveal where your goodness meets my life. As I expand my own compassion and share with others in need, I know that you will fill me up and provide for me and mine. God of abundance, you are my Father, and I trust you. You are generous; I don't have to fear your response when I reach out for help. Thank you.

I have been freely given so much in the Lord, so I will freely share the bounty of my life with others. I will count every sacrifice as a gift for God's grace. I am learning to love more freely, and it is expanding my experience as well as my understanding.

Always Available

The Lord is a refuge for the oppressed,
a stronghold in times of trouble.

PSALM 9:9 NIV

Lord, thank you for being available every moment through your Spirit. There isn't a time I turn to you where I find that you are too busy. Even when I can't perceive your presence, I know you are with me because you are faithful to your Word. You do not turn those away who look to you for help. You don't close yourself off from those who run to you for refuge. You are a stronghold in times of trouble.

Rise up on behalf of your people and turn the tide of our battles. Bring breakthrough where we are closed in. Bring light where there is darkness. Please do your work as we run to hide in your faithfulness.

All who are oppressed can find their refuge in God Almighty. I will not side with those who are looking to dominate the vulnerable. I stand with the Lord, and I will be a place of refuge for those who need it.

Rest in the Almighty

Those who live in the shelter of the Most High
will find rest in the shadow of the Almighty.

PSALM 91:1 NLT

Almighty God, there are a million ways to get lost in the
tyrannical demands of modern life, but that is not the way
of your kingdom. As I lay aside lists of requirements to be
successful in the world's eyes, I turn to you. I will not give
up the work that is mine, but I will not do what is beyond
me. I choose to rest in your faithfulness as I trust your
power at work in me.

You did not tell us to work incessantly. I long to learn the
rhythms of rest that you put in place so that I am free to
fill up on peace, fun, and true, deep respite. Thank you for
recreation and for hobbies. Thank you for small delights
and the pleasure of slowing down and tuning in.

*I will do the work that is mine today, and I will leave the rest
for another day. I will let myself off the hook, whatever that
looks like today, and connect with myself and loved ones in
meaningful ways.*

My Rescue

The LORD says, "I will rescue those who love me.
I will protect those who trust in my name."

PSALM 91:14 NLT

Rescuer, I love you. I trust you. These are not just words to repeat from your Word; they are the echoes of my heart's desire. To love you and trust you completely is my deepest wish. I choose to draw near even as you beckon me.

You see the things that I can't control. You know the worries that light up my mind at night. You know the troubles I face, and you faithfully keep me safe. Do what only you can do and minister peace to my heart and mind. I run into the shelter of your presence now. Please keep me there by your grace. I trust you more than I trust anyone else.

I declare that God is worthy of my love and my trust. He is my Savior in every area of need. He does not require me to be perfect in love; he has fulfilled that requirement. Over and over again, I will bring my attention back to him as I offer him my heart.

I Will Trust

I will say of the LORD,
"He is my refuge and my fortress;
My God, in Him I will trust."

PSALM 91:2 NKJV

Lord God, when the storms of this world pick up and the winds and threaten to blow me away, may I be found in the fortress of your love. You are my strong tower, the place I run into when I have nowhere else to turn.

Thank you for not despising my calls to you. You are a ready help. It doesn't matter if the last time we talked was ten minutes ago or ten years ago. You never turn me away. Today I will trust you with everything that comes my way, and I won't stop trusting you. May your faithfulness shine like the noonday sun.

I declare that I throw all my trust into God today. He is the faithful one, the God who never tires or wearies. He never grows sleepy or distracted. He is my attentive and powerful help.

Sheltered by Faithfulness

He will cover you with his feathers.
He will shelter you with his wings.
His faithful promises are your armor and protection.

PSALM 91:4 NLT

Everlasting God, from age to age, you remain the same. You offer mercy to those who look to you, and your generosity is unmatched. There are no strings attached to your love. You shelter the vulnerable, and you make a way where there was none.

You are the same God who parted the seas so that the Israelites could escape their captors on dry land. You are the same God who fought on behalf of his people. You are the same God who unlocked chains and opened prison doors. What you have done, you continue to do in loyal love. Increase my faith as you continue to move in faithfulness.

The shelter of God's presence isn't reserved for the ultra-religious. It is not a place for the supposed holy elite. It is for all who turn to him. He covers me with his feathers, and he shelters me with his wings. His promises are my armor and protection.

Sweet Relief

When anxiety was great within me,
your consolation brought me joy.

PSALM 94:19 NIV

Prince of Peace, you have known me at my worst and at my best. You have seen me seething with anger, flooded by worry, and overwhelmed by fear. You have seen me full of hope, daring to delight in the moment, and laughing with those I love. You are the same, no matter what my emotional state.

When anxiety sends me spinning and I worry about the unknowns ahead, be my consolation. Be my great peace and calm my frayed nerves. Slow down my thoughts with the peace of your presence. Bring relief to my mind and heart as you offer me your perspective that is unworried, brave, and confident in love. You are the only one who can do this for me. I trust you.

The Lord is my comfort and my strength. He brings relief when he is near, and he is always near. I will turn my attention to him now and drink up the refreshing waters of his presence. Joy and hope are mine.